Cambridge English
Advanced
Result

Workbook Resource Pack with Key

Kathy Gude
Lynda Edwards

OXFORD
UNIVERSITY PRESS

OXFORD
UNIVERSITY PRESS

Great Clarendon Street, Oxford, OX2 6DP, United Kingdom

Oxford University Press is a department of the University of Oxford. It furthers the University's objective of excellence in research, scholarship, and education by publishing worldwide. Oxford is a registered trade mark of Oxford University Press in the UK and in certain other countries

© Oxford University Press 2014

The moral rights of the author have been asserted

First published in 2014

2018 2017 2016 2015 2014

10 9 8 7 6 5 4 3 2

No unauthorized photocopying

All rights reserved. No part of this publication may be reproduced, stored in a retrieval system, or transmitted, in any form or by any means, without the prior permission in writing of Oxford University Press, or as expressly permitted by law, by licence or under terms agreed with the appropriate reprographics rights organization. Enquiries concerning reproduction outside the scope of the above should be sent to the ELT Rights Department, Oxford University Press, at the address above

You must not circulate this work in any other form and you must impose this same condition on any acquirer

Links to third party websites are provided by Oxford in good faith and for information only. Oxford disclaims any responsibility for the materials contained in any third party website referenced in this work

ISBN: 978 0 19 451241 1

Printed in China

This book is printed on paper from certified and well-managed sources

ACKNOWLEDGEMENTS

The publisher would like to thank the following for their permission to reproduce photographs: Alamy pp.14 (boy with tooth), 15 (FocusJapan), 20 (icy road), 28 (swordfish/Jeff Rotman), 48 (Lebrecht Music and Arts Photo Library), 50, 52, 76 (recycling bins, landfill/Chris Gomersall), 80; Corbis pp.11 (snowmobiles/Dan Burton/Robert Harding Specialist Stock), 14 (Uluru/Dallas and John Heaton/Free Agents Limited), 21 (Carol & Mike Werner/Visuals Unlimited), 25 (woman with turtle), 28 (springbok/Ralph Lee Hopkins/National Geographic Society, archer fish/Kim Taylor/Nature Picture Library), 34 (children having lunch), 35, 41 (Ray Juno), 46, 72 (Tom & Dee Ann McCarthy), 75 (Paul Almasy), 76 (women carrying/Nigel Pavitt/John Warburton-Lee Photography Ltd); Getty pp.5 (Karen Moskowitz), 7 (Jinx Jinx), 20 (couple/Sean Justice), 33 (Philip and Karen Smith), 58, 60 (policeman/Matt Cardy), 81; Oxford University Press pp.14 (man eating), 16 (apple), 17, 27, 29, 40 (carrots), 60 (woman), 65 (big button), 69 (all); Rex Features pp.36 (Catwoman/Warner Bros/Everett, Lara Croft/Moviestore Collection), 37 (Elektra/Snap Stills), 40 (Popeye/Everett Collection), 44 and 45 (*A Field in England*/Picturehouse Entertainment/courtesy Everett Collection), 54 (David James), 61 (Warner Bros/Everett); Shutterstock pp.8, 9, 11 (reindeer), 16 (scientist), 25 (woman with diving equipment), 26, 28 (ant, termite mound, cheetah), 30, 34 (yoga, woman in park), 39, 47, 49, 51, 56, 57, 60 (teen boy), 64 (buttons), 65 (zip), 66, 67, 68, 70 (all), 71 (both), 74 (both).

Illustrations by: Gill Button pp.13, 53, 73, 79; Melvyn Evans pp.18, 19, 59.

Picture research: Alison Wright

The authors and publisher are grateful to those who have given permission to reproduce the following extracts and adaptations of copyright material: p.4 Adapted extract from "Better and Better" by Caroline Righton, The Guardian, 23 April 2005. Copyright Guardian News & Media Ltd 2005. p.8 Adapted extract from "What are friends for?" by Jenni Russell, The Guardian, 24 January 2005. Copyright Guardian News & Media Ltd 2005. p.10 Adapted extract from "Sled Time Story" by Jenny Diski, The Observer, 30 January 2005. Copyright Guardian News & Media Ltd 2005. p.15 Adapted extract from "Snow and Ice Festival, Japan", www.lonelyplanet.com, accessed 19 October 2004. Reproduced with permission from the Lonely Planet website www.lonelyplanet.com © 2004 Lonely Planet. p.17 Extract from "The Advantages & Disadvantages of Genetically Modified Food: Both Sides of the Debate" by Sonal Panse, edited by Paul Arnold, www.brighthub.com, 4 August 2013. Reproduced by permission of Sonal Panse. p.16 Adapted extract from Genetically Modified Foods: Harmful or Helpful?" by Deborah B. Whitman, www.csa.com, released April 2000. © 2013, ProQuest. All rights reserved. p.21 Adapted extract from "The power of darkness" by Hugh Wilson, *The Guardian*, 15 March 2005. Copyright Guardian News & Media Ltd 2005. p.24 Adapted extract from "Take the plunge…" by Dottie Monaghan, *Woman & Home*. © Woman & Home/IPC+ Syndication. p.28 Adapted extract from "The Animal Olympics", *Daily Express*, 11 July 2005. Reproduced by permission of Express Newspapers. p.29 Adapted extract from "Among the giants" by Sebastião Salgado/Amazonas Images, The Guardian, 7 May 2005. Reproduced by permission of NB Pictures. p.34 Adapted extract from "Out to lunch" by Bibi van der Zee, *The Guardian*, 24 January 2005. Copyright Guardian News & Media Ltd 2005. p.35 Adapted extract from "A quick workout can do you as much good as a long one" by Daily Mail Reporter, *Daily Mail*, 24 March 2005. Reproduced by permission of Solo Syndication. p.36 Adapted extract from "I need a heroine" by Tanya Gold, *The Guardian*, 1 July 2005. Copyright Guardian News & Media Ltd 2005. p.40 Speakers 1, 2, 3 and 5: Adapted extracts from "Food Myths", Slimming World's Online programme, accessed 2006. Reproduced by permission of Slimming World. p.41 Adapted extract from "Giant mirror to light up village" by Barbara McMahon, *The Guardian*, 14 September 2005. Copyright Guardian News & Media Ltd 2005. p.44 Adapted extract from "Film reviews: A Field in England, The Bling Ring and more" by Nigel Andrews, from the Financial Times, July 4, 2013. © The Financial Times Limited 2013. All Rights Reserved. p.44 Adapted extract from "Film Review: A Field in England – Ben Wheatley's glorious low-budget Civil War drama" by Geoffrey Macnab, The Independent, 5 July 2013. Reproduced by permission of Independent Print Limited. p.44 Extract adapted from "Review: A Field in England" by Peter Bradshaw, www.theguardian.com, 4 July 2013. Copyright Guardian News & Media Ltd 2013. p.48 Adapted extract from The Hunt for Amazing Treasures by Sondra Farrell Bazrod (Random House, 1999). Reproduced by permission of Sondra Farrell Bazrod. p.51 Abridged extract from A History of the World by Andrew Marr, Pan Books, London (2013). © Andrew Marr 2013. Reproduced by permission of Pan Macmillan. p.56 Adapted extract from "Families and other criminals" by Susanna Yager, *The Telegraph*, April 2005. © Telegraph Media Group Limited 2005. p.60 Adapted extract from "Tough love" by Rebecca Smithers, *The Guardian*, 21 June 2005. Copyright Guardian News & Media Ltd 2005. p.61 Adapted extract from "Review of *Ocean's Twelve*" by Mark Dujsik, Mark Reviews Movies (www.markreviewsmovies.com). © by Mark Dujsik. All rights reserved. p.64 Adapted extract from "The tiger's teeth" by Jonathan Watts, *The Guardian*, 25 May 2005. Copyright Guardian News & Media Ltd 2005. p.70 Adapted extract from "The power of photography: time, mortality and memory" by Blake Morrison, Mary McCartney, Steve Pyke, Grayson Perry, Katie Mitchell, Sean O'Hagan, Jemima Kiss, Louise Wilson and Adrian Searle, The Guardian, 19 May 2013. Copyright Guardian News & Media Ltd 2013. Reproduced by permission of Guardian News and Media Ltd and Mary McCartney. p.74 Adapted extract from "SoYouWanna fake an appreciation for art?", http://www.soyouwanna.com. © Demand Media, Inc. p.75 Adapted extract from "Previously hidden Salvador Dali paintings go under the hammer" by Mark Brown, The Guardian, 15 May 2013. Copyright Guardian News & Media Ltd 2013. p.76 Adapted extract from "Feel-good factor: But will it save the planet" by John Vidal & Paul Brown, *The Guardian*, 20 May 2005. Copyright Guardian News & Media Ltd 2005. p.80 Adapted extract from "Ripe for change" by various contributors, *The Guardian*, 30 June 2005. Copyright Guardian News & Media Ltd 2005. p.81 Adapted extract from "Battle of the bag" by Caroline Williams, *New Scientist*, 11 September 2004. © 2004 Reed Business Information – UK. All rights reserved. Distributed by Tribune Content Agency.

Sources: pp.20, 54, 55, 68, 69 www.bbc.co.uk

Although every effort has been made to trace and contact copyright holders before publication, this has not been possible in some cases. We apologize for any apparent infringement of copyright and if notified, the publisher will be pleased to rectify any errors or omissions at the earliest opportunity.

1 What are you like?
page 4

2 Customs and traditions
page 10

3 Looking ahead
page 16

Review (Units 1–3)
page 22

4 Into the wild
page 24

5 Health matters
page 30

6 Would you believe it?
page 36

Review (Units 4–6)
page 42

7 Traces of the past
page 44

8 The big issues
page 50

9 It's a crime
page 56

Review (Units 7–9)
page 62

10 Buying and selling
page 64

11 Entertainment or art?
page 70

12 A changing world
page 76

Review (Units 10–12)
page 82

Writing
page 84

Speaking
page 90

Key
page 95

Using the Workbook MultiROM
page 111

What are you like?

Reading Part 5 Multiple choice

1 Read the article quickly and decide which sentence (a, b or c) is the best summary.

a Dealing with problems in your life.
b Finding out how to take things easy.
c Learning to be more positive.

2 Read the text again and for questions 1–6, choose the answer (A, B, C or D) which you think fits best.

1 What does the writer advise people to do before getting up in the morning?

  A Calmly contemplate their day ahead.
  B Organise their routine to maximise their time.
  C Decide which undesirable activity they could dispense with.
  D Reject the idea of having to fulfil their obligations successfully.

Better and better

TAKE A COUPLE OF MINUTES to lie still in bed and reflect on the day ahead. Do you feel cheerful or fed up, excited or bored? Or do you, perhaps, feel nothing? Go on, prod your subconscious to consider your
5 situation. Unless you get pleasure from living a passive and non-eventful life, having a non-committal attitude can actually be as bad as being pessimistic. So if, as you walk yourself through the events of the day ahead, you feel pretty average about things, then try and aim
10 higher. It will mean that you get much more out of life. So there you are, lying in bed. Picture yourself showering, making breakfast, catching the bus, attending meetings, shopping, cooking supper, watching TV and finally getting into bed. Did your spirits sink at the thought of any of it?
15 If so, pluck what it was out of the timetable and examine it more closely. Is it a must-do, non-negotiable event? For instance, you may not mind the idea of going to work but hate your job or the daily commute. Find out what options you have to make changes or find alternatives.
20 In the meantime, come up with a strong and confident affirming statement about the person you wish to be and the way you wish to tackle these life challenges.

Once you have a clear picture of the things in your life that make you feel low, either eliminate, minimise or
25 improve them and the way you manage them. If getting everyone organised in the morning is a nightmare, you need to apply some lateral thought to the process. Encourage everybody to help with the morning routine. Make everyone responsible for some parts of their own
30 organisation. If everyone is leading busy lives in the household, it makes no sense for one person to be a martyr. Be realistic about your own stamina and stress limits and appreciate the importance of keeping yourself fit and happy. Agree new regimes with family members
35 or housemates as a sensible training exercise, and stick with it until everyone takes their equal share. Instead of feeling miserable about your chores and responsibilities, adopt a positive approach and acknowledge that they are an essential component of life.

2 The writer suggests dealing with difficult aspects of our home lives by
   A freeing up more time to handle them more effectively.
   B delegating some responsibilities to others.
   C learning to control stress by taking more exercise.
   D asking for outside help to relieve pressures.

3 The writer initially implies that adopting a realistic attitude towards life can
   A have a counterproductive effect on our lives.
   B encourage us to look on the bright side of life.
   C enable us to find solutions to our problems.
   D help us be more analytical in our approach to life.

4 By using the expression 'tune into' in line 44 the writer is suggesting that this is something that you
   A do regularly.
   B really enjoy.
   C may find difficult.
   D won't easily forget.

5 The writer justifies having a positive outlook on the day by saying it will
   A make the outcome of our day more predictable.
   B help us blank out the less desirable events in our lives.
   C give us renewed energy to face up to problems in life.
   D reinforce our appreciation of what makes life worthwhile.

6 According to the writer, how should we react to having had a bad day?
   A Focus on the one positive thing that happened, however insignificant.
   B Try to communicate our feelings about it to another person in a positive way.
   C Tell ourselves it is perfectly acceptable to feel down after a day like that.
   D Stay positive and believe that tomorrow will be a better day.

40 Pessimism, doubt and negativity can often disguise themselves as realism. Facing up to the facts can sometimes be healthy but it's essential not to poison hope and optimism with negative thoughts. Observing how you think is vital. You really need to tune into
45 hearing those negative waves as soon as they start and see a more positive alternative view. To find this perspective, you may need to examine closely the experience or subject of your attention. Be curious and interested in life, the things and the people that make
50 up your day. Be resolute that you will find a positive in everything and everyone.

The logical rationale for having a positive attitude is compelling. Nobody knows for sure what each day will bring and whether its end will mark a personal triumph
55 or disaster. Make yourself work out what good things will happen. Today could be the day you meet your soul mate, or when you are praised or promoted. Carry a list and photographs of things in your life that are rewarding or make you feel happy. This can include
60 loved ones, favourite flowers, song tracks, a cutting from a newspaper that made you laugh, or a theatre ticket that reminds you of a wonderful occasion. If you need reminding that good things do happen, take this collection out and relive fond memories and thoughts.

65 Even if today has been a bad day, you needn't go to bed depressed because your optimism didn't pay off. Why? Well, because tomorrow is another day. In the same way that a single look or a sour comment can instantly kill a feeling, so a bubble of optimism arising from even the
70 most minor triumph will eventually get bigger if you refuse to let yourself look on the dark side. That is the great thing about life.

Unit 1 5

Vocabulary

Feelings

1 Put these words into a suitable category below. Check your answers in a dictionary. Then use them to complete sentences a–i.

> depressed   confident   cheerful   fed up
> curious   pessimistic realistic optimistic
> moody   realistic   bored   excited

Positive: ....

Negative: ....

Neutral: ....

a I'm .... with everyone asking me to do things for them all the time. Nobody ever says thank you or helps me.

b Bob has a rather .... attitude towards the future of our planet. He's convinced global warming will destroy the Earth very soon.

c We must be .... and do everything possible to improve the transport facilities in the town.

d Zeb seems very .... He wasn't nervous about making that speech to the whole college.

e You're not being very .... about our plans for the summer. We just couldn't afford to go on holiday to a place like that.

f You never know how Ann will feel – happy, sad – she can be very ....

g I'm .... to know how many students failed the exam, aren't you?

h I'm so .... ! I'm going on a two-week holiday tomorrow morning!

i I'm very rarely .... I can always find something interesting to do.

Meanings of *get*

2 Match the expressions in italics in a–h with one of the meanings in brackets.

a If you want to *get more out of* life, try to be more organised. (create or invent more from/extract or obtain more from)

b I'd like to *get out of* going to the party tonight but I don't see how I can. (avoid doing something/persuade someone not to do something)

c I'm really struggling with this grammar. I just don't *get* it. (understand/like)

d We ought to be going home. It's *getting on for* midnight. (past/nearly)

e It's no good *getting* upset about what happened. There's nothing you can do about it now. (making/becoming)

f The students *get on with* each other very well. (make progress/have a good relationship)

g I think it's time we *got down to* doing our homework. (finished/began)

h This argument is *getting* us *nowhere*. Let's just agree to disagree. (achieving nothing/leading us in the wrong direction)

3 Complete sentences a–g using a suitable expression with *get* in the correct form. Then use a dictionary to find two more expressions with *get* and note their meaning.

a Do you .... Kate? I really don't know her.

b We need to .... doing all the jobs in the house that we haven't done for ages.

c This consultation process is .... It's virtually impossible to please everybody.

d It's .... 6 o'clock. Great! It's nearly time to finish work and go home!

e I want to try to .... college, you know, join some clubs or learn a new language.

f Try not to .... offended by what Mary said. I'm sure she didn't really mean it.

g How can we .... visiting the Browns this weekend? I'd rather stay at home!

Unit 1

Grammar

Review of verb patterns

1 Complete conversations 1–6 by putting the verb in brackets in the correct form.

1. A: One of my colleagues wanted me .... (buy) a mobile phone like hers.
   B: But yours is quite new. I really object to .... (change) something for the sake of it.

2. A: We could put off .... (make) a decision about installing machinery until next year.
   B: That might mean we need to resort to .... (spend) a huge amount on maintaining the existing machinery.

3. A: Has it always been company policy to avoid .... (give) a refund on sales goods?
   B: Yes. You can issue a credit note but you must insist on .... (see) the receipt.

4. A: I don't recall .... (receive) any notification about the change in dates.
   B: I'm afraid it was a last minute amendment. I do apologise for .... (not/inform) you.

5. A: The Wrights never stop .... (boast) about their children's achievements.
   B: Perhaps you ought to .... (mention) the fact that they have already told you!

6. A: Bill can't stand .... (commute) for three hours every day.
   B: Maybe you should advise him .... (look) for a job closer to home?

2 Complete these sentences using a suitable verb below in the infinitive form with or without *to*.

strike   complete   feel   provide
solve   accept   inform   enter

a. Several residents heard someone .... the building in the early hours of the morning.
b. The management refuse .... responsibility for any damage to property on the premises.
c. Under the terms of the contract, we agree .... the work in a period of three weeks.
d. The letter was written in such an aggressive tone that it made me .... angry.
e. Sam's tutor offered .... him with some extra help with his thesis.
f. Can anyone help .... this confusion about transportation costs?
g. The baggage handlers at the airport threatened .... if their demands were not met.
h. We regret .... you that the item you ordered is no longer available.

3 Match the sentence halves using the prepositions below and the correct form of the verb in brackets. Three of the prepositions are <u>not</u> needed.

at   for   on   of   from   by

a. Please don't blame me ...
b. I can't believe Anne's supervisor actually accused her ...
c. The police praised everyone ...
d. Most hotels try to discourage guests ...
e. Voters will never forgive the government ...
f. Officials tried to prevent the spectators ...
g. That scruffy old rucksack reminds me ...

1. (smoke) in their bedrooms.
2. (forget) what you should have remembered yourself.
3. (not/live) up to their election promises.
4. (steal) her own office stationery.
5. (rush) onto the pitch at the end of the game.
6. (travel) across Europe when I was a student.
7. (not/panic) during the bomb scare.

Unit 1

Listening Part 4 Multiple matching

1 Read the instructions and questions for 2, which are about people discussing friendship. Which statements reflect your own opinions or experiences?

2 🎧 Listen to five short extracts and complete the exam task.

For 1–5, choose from A–H the people's attitudes towards friendships.

A The only people I feel I can make demands on are my friends.
B I think I can honestly say that I have never really had a best friend.
C I expect my friends to place our friendship above everything.
D We often give friends a one-sided impression of our true selves.
E Friends are people you can invite to a dinner party at the last minute.
F I always take advantage of opportunities to meet people.
G My friendships mean far more to me than even my job.
H I socialise with people of a similar background to myself.

Speaker 1 [1]
Speaker 2 [2]
Speaker 3 [3]
Speaker 4 [4]
Speaker 5 [5]

For 6–10, choose from A–H what upsets the people about friendships.

A not being able to rely on friends in times of trouble
B being bothered by someone who won't accept the friendship is over
C constantly being forced to make new friends
D realising that your friendship is no longer of any value
E dealing with friends' emotional problems
F losing touch with people who have been your friends since childhood
G being let down by friends at work
H knowing their position in the group is what matters to your friends

Speaker 1 [6]
Speaker 2 [7]
Speaker 3 [8]
Speaker 4 [9]
Speaker 5 [10]

Unit 1

Use of English   Part 3 Word formation

1 Read the article below about interviews. How does the author advise people to perfect their interview technique?
 a in front of a mirror
 b with someone they know well
 c with an expert in the field

2 Read the text again and complete gaps 1–8 with words formed from those in capitals below.

Preparing for your first interview

Before going to an interview, it is (0) ....*advisable*.... to go through a mock interview. This will enable you to try out your technique and answers live. It is also a chance to receive constructive feedback that is (1) .... in improving your interview style and general (2) .... Just one mock interview will result in a (3) .... improvement in your skills. Why? For the same reason that a (4) .... doesn't exist while still on paper or floating in your head. It only exists when you give it (5) .... The first time you give it in front of an audience, it will be nothing like the one you prepared. So, seek out a (6) .... and have the practice session filmed. You will probably find that when you play the recording back you get a completely different impression of yourself and of your (7) .... For maximum effect, revisit your answers and go through a second mock interview. This should help you cope with any (8) .... and will give you more confidence.

0	ADVISE	3	NOTICE	6	PROFESSION
1	BENEFIT	4	SPEAK	7	RESPOND
2	PRESENT	5	ORAL	8	EASE

3 Write the correct words for a–h.

Example
a noun form of the verb 'improve' ..*improvement*..

 a two noun forms of the verb 'advise' ....
 b an adjective and two nouns formed from the verb 'present' ....
 c the adverb form of the noun/verb 'notice' ....
 d two noun forms of the verb 'speak' ....
 e another noun form of the noun 'profession' ....
 f the positive and negative adjective forms of the noun 'impression' ....
 g the positive and negative adjective forms of the verb 'respond' ....
 h two adjective forms of the noun 'confidence' ....

Unit 1

Customs and traditions

Reading Part 7 Gapped text

1 Read the text and paragraphs A–G quickly and find out:
a who the Sami are.
b what annual custom the writer takes part in.
c if the writer enjoyed the experience.

2 Read the whole text again and choose from the paragraphs A–G the one which fits each gap (1–6). There is one extra paragraph which you do not need to use.

ARCTIC ADVE

I wanted to experience life under the midday moon. A heated log cabin and maybe a sauna, in Sweden's far north, meditating on the loss of light and the loneliness, in a drawn-out, snowy, winter world. And that's what I said to my editor, so I was packed off to Övre Soppero with photographer Mark. 'Oh, it's never dark up here,' our host Per-Nils Päiviö insisted when we met him and his wife, Britt-Marie, who was preparing a reindeer stew.

1 ☐

The next two days and nights in the warmth of the cabin and the traditional circular hut covered in turf, with wood-burning stoves – and a sauna – were cosy. Informative, too, as – over breakfast with pancakes – I was given a thorough education in the ancient and barely altered life of the reindeer-herding Sami people of northern Sweden. Just as I was beginning to relax, I was introduced to 'my' reindeer. I was handed the reins along with some sparse instructions: pull left for faster, right for stop.

2 ☐

Tonight Per-Nils was taking us by snowmobile to the huts where the families lived over the three-day round-up. But he, Mark and I were spending the night in a 'lavvu', guarding the reindeer. Back home I had discovered that this word, which had appeared on my itinerary, meant a tent. I imagined a warm tourist tent. But now alarm bells began to ring.

3 ☐

Somehow, I survived the lack of sleep. Then the round-up began. Everyone revved up their snowmobiles and spread out, surrounding the reindeer. Dogs barked, people shouted, and 7,000 reindeer ran in the desired direction: into a large corral, where they were then herded by people on foot towards the narrow passage; then about 70 animals were funnelled through a small circular space with gates to 'family' paddocks.

4 ☐

I declined to wrestle with a reindeer, but Mark put down his camera and grabbed one shouting, 'It's ours', as he was dragged across the corral floor. I simply begged for a bed with walls that night, and maybe even a jacuzzi.

We had another magical ride back on the snowmobile and then a car to Kiruna, the home of the Sami parliament and the Swedish iron ore mine, which has utterly changed the traditional herding land and threatens the Sami way of life.

5 ☐

After a day off, I visited a local school. The Sami pupils take lessons in their own language and study skills and traditions that are rapidly being forgotten. The youngsters were looking to the future and making plans for their lives beyond reindeer herding.

6 ☐

Even I know how privileged I was to participate in that. And the extra hands can certainly be useful: Mark apparently was an asset, and me? Well, now I've warmed up a bit, I am grateful for the experience. I just hope I didn't make life too difficult for my hosts.

Unit 2

A ⁵⁵ But for me, the best thing was that it had the Hotel Ralleran, a wooden building devotedly restored, and a shrine to simplicity. It had beautiful, pale-timbered walls, wooden floors, light, space, a ⁶⁰ comfortable bed and a jacuzzi!

B I sat in the family paddock by a log fire and choked on wood smoke. 'Ah', a fur-encased elderly lady laughed. 'The smoke follows you. It means you'll be rich.' Or so her ⁶⁵ daughter translated. What she probably said was: 'Who is this stranger?'

C Dinner was delicious and marked our introduction to Swedish Lapland as guests of the Sami, the indigenous people who ⁷⁰ were here long before anyone else arrived. 'Snow. Northern lights. And you can go into the forest in December and you hardly need a torch', he commented. Despite my reservations, I was intrigued and actually ⁷⁵ keen to start our 'adventure'.

D Yet they showed a demonstrable desire to keep their heritage alive. That's why the Sami are inviting visitors to experience their traditions and so try to sustain their ⁸⁰ reindeer-herding life.

E My fears turned out to be justified. The Sami tepee had a layer of reindeer skins over the bare, snow-covered, lumpy earth. The gap around the bottom let plenty of fresh air ⁸⁵ in. I spent most of the time perched on my elbows, staring at the embers of the fire.

F The reindeer took over immediately, either sauntering along or racing his mate. My performance lost the respect of the guides, ⁹⁰ but they were kind and excitedly started talking about tomorrow's agenda. They had brought together the 7,000 reindeer of the district, and tomorrow we would participate in the annual separation of the herds into ⁹⁵ family groups. This is done according to the signs on the ears of the calves to allocate the winter grazing.

G My job was to head off stragglers and escapees. This is done by flapping the arms ¹⁰⁰ up and down and hooting. Even the most desultory flap, I discovered, persuades a wayward reindeer to rejoin the crowd.

Vocabulary

Words with similar meanings

1 Match one word from each pair in a–f with the definition provided and then write a definition for the other word. Use a dictionary to help you.

a imaginary/imaginative
    having or showing new and exciting ideas
    ....

b exhausting/exhaustive
    making you feel very tired
    ....

c conscious/conscientious
    awake and able to see, hear and think
    ....

d satisfying/satisfactory
    good enough for a particular purpose
    ....

e sensible/sensitive
    aware of and able to understand other people and their feelings
    ....

f indigenous/indignant
    feeling or showing anger or annoyance
    ....

2 Use words from 1 to complete these sentences.

a Fortunately, your performance was .... and you passed the exam.
b Samson is a very .... writer and always constructs an intricate and fascinating plot.
c The government's survey into unemployment is the most .... document of its kind.
d I can't believe Chris cheated in the exam! He's usually so .... !
e Our school is .... to problems facing new students and we aim to support them fully.
f You have every right to be .... I would be furious if anyone said that about me!

Compound nouns

3 Circle the one word on the right which <u>cannot</u> be combined with a–e to form a compound noun. Then scan through the entries for a–e in a dictionary to find more compound nouns.

a hand   book/shake/bar/basin
b film   crew/goer/picture/script
c news   agent/flash/data/reader
d side   effect/mark/track/street
e work   hour/shop/place/out

4 Make compound nouns by matching a–e with 1–5. There may be more than one answer. Check your ideas in a dictionary.

a take   1 through
b turn   2 over
c set   3 out
d hand   4 back
e break   5 down

5 Use the compound nouns you formed in 4 to complete these sentences. Then say what each compound noun means in the context of a–h.

a The surprisingly low .... at the tennis tournament was due to torrential rain.
b An unsuccessful .... bid was made by an unknown investor last year.
c Research into hereditary illness has resulted in a welcome .... for scientists.
d A .... will be distributed to all students at the end of the lecture.
e Unfortunately, there has been a temporary .... in the peace negotiations.
f It is reputed that the oil company has an annual .... of forty million dollars.
g The .... of power to the newly elected government took place yesterday.
h There has been a .... at the prison – three inmates are thought to have escaped.

Grammar

Gerunds and infinitives

1 Complete gaps 1–8 with the correct form of the verbs below. You may need to add a preposition.

> be   waste   establish   cope   send
> travel   go   expand

Tim wasn't looking forward 1 .... on his first business trip to Latvia in the middle of winter. He wasn't very keen 2 .... in icy conditions and he'd never been very good 3 .... with cold temperatures. In any case, he didn't believe 4 .... time making personal visits when a phone call or email would do just as well. He objected 5 .... told what to do, but his boss had insisted 6 .... him there for a brief meeting. The company had been thinking 7 .... into that part of the world for some time and had already succeeded 8 .... contacts in Central and Eastern Europe.

2 Match sentence halves a–f with 1–6 and put the verbs in brackets in the correct form.

a   Did Sally actually manage …
b   Is it true that Sam threatened …
c   What do you hope …
d   I don't think we should risk …
e   Would you prefer …
f   The accused man denied …

1   (do) in ten years' time?
2   (convince) Andrea to watch that horror film?
3   (drive) to the airport in case there's a traffic jam.
4   (have) a vegetarian dish for your main course?
5   (resign) if he wasn't given a salary increase?
6   (steal) the money but no one believed him.

Relative clauses

3 Combine the sentences in a–g using a relative pronoun and, where necessary, a preposition.

a   This is the old car. William used it to travel all over Europe.
b   The new train can reach speeds of 300 km per hour. The train's design is certainly innovative.
c   The Welsh mountains are very beautiful. I spent most of my childhood there.
d   We met other employees. Most had been with the company for a few years.
e   Winning the World Cup was one of those wonderful moments. You feel perfectly happy.
f   The film star is the subject of much gossip. She will be at the premiere in New York tomorrow.
g   The accident happened. We cannot explain it.

Winter in Latvia

Unit 2

Listening

Part 1 Multiple choice

1 Answer these questions which relate to the extracts in 2 below.

   a What are the most popular traditional dishes in your country?
   b Were there any particular customs from your childhood that you enjoyed?
   c Which are the most popular tourist attractions in your country?

2 🎧 Read questions 1–6 below before you listen to the three different extracts. Then listen and choose the answer (A, B or C) which fits best according to what you hear.

extract one
You hear part of an interview with a woman who is writing a series of guides about traditional food.

1 What information do the guides give?
   A introductions to the leading chefs of the area
   B the reasons why certain meals became popular
   C details of locally grown produce used in dishes

2 What is the writer's reason for writing the guides?
   A to teach a new generation of cooks
   B to develop her experience as a writer
   C to help tourists find authentic traditional food

extract two
You hear two people talking about customs from their childhood.

3 What do the speakers believe about the Tooth Fairy?
   A It can only visit when you sleep.
   B It is a purely British custom.
   C It helps a new tooth grow.

4 The woman continued the custom with her children because
   A children's teeth are important.
   B children should have beliefs like this.
   C customs shouldn't be broken.

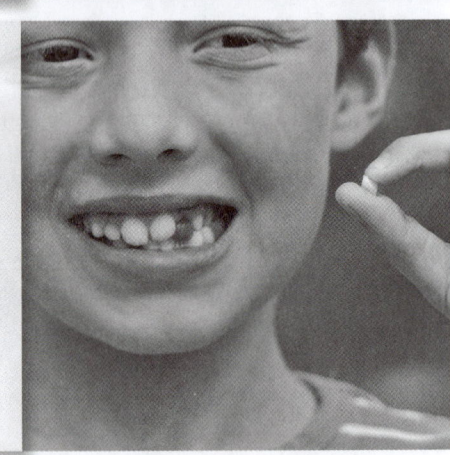

extract three
You hear part of an interview with a tour guide from Australia.

5 The tour guide describes Ayers Rock as special because it is
   A a different colour from normal rock.
   B bigger than any other rock on earth.
   C a major visitor attraction for Australia.

6 Visitors are not allowed to climb Ayers Rock because
   A its history should be respected.
   B tours make it overcrowded.
   C there isn't a safe track.

Use of English

Part 2 Open cloze

1 Read the text below quickly, ignoring the gaps, and find out how the Japanese festival started.

2 For questions 1–8, read the text again and think of the word which best fits each gap.

STATUES OF SAPPORO

The capital of Japan's northernmost island attracts visitors every year in February. (0) ...*Despite*... this being the coldest time of the year, visitors flock to the city, which transforms (1) .... into a dream world of glittering snow sculptures. More than two million people come to marvel (2) .... these frosted creations.

The festival began in 1950, (3) .... two students fashioned six snow statues in Odori Park. Five years (4) .... , members of Sapporo's Defence Force sowed the seeds of the now world-famous festival by building the first statue which was megalithic in (5) .... proportions. Snow sculpting might sound (6) .... an easy skill, but it takes a lot of patience and artistic talent. First, a wooden structure is built and large blocks of snow are hammered into place around it. Once positioned, the blocks are hosed with water to freeze them together. It is only (7) .... that the painstaking job of sculpting can begin.

The result is a crystal-like dreamscape of well-known images, (8) .... as those of famous buildings and people.

Part 4 Key word transformation

3 Rewrite the second sentence in a–e keeping the meaning the same. Use three to six words, including the word given.

a The majority of people like to observe customs and traditions.
   FAVOUR
   The majority of people ....
   .... customs and traditions.

b We are not often invited to meetings at the college.
   ACCUSTOMED
   We are not ....
   to meetings at the college.

c The results show attendance has risen dramatically during the last year.
   IN
   The results show a ....
   .... during the last year.

d My sister finds commuting every day really annoying.
   PUT
   It's difficult for my sister ....
   .... commuting every day.

e The number of participants in the snow festival has reached an all-time high.
   MUCH
   The number of participants in the snow festival is ....
   .... been.

Unit 2 15

Looking ahead

Reading

Part 6 Cross-text multiple matching

1 Quickly read the four extracts opposite and answer the following questions.
  a Which writer feels that GM foods might solve more problems than they create?
  b Which three writers are sceptical about the long-term effects of GM foods?

2 Read the extracts again. For questions 1–4, choose from the writers A–D. The writers may be chosen more than once.

Which writer, A, B, C or D:

shares the opinion of writer C regarding the feelings the subject
of GM food arouses?   1 …

has a different opinion from the other writers about the justification
for developing GM foods?   2 …

takes a similar view to writer B regarding reservations about the
development of GM foods?   3 …

shares the same opinion as writer A as regards the importance to
everyone of the issues surrounding GM foods?   4 …

3 Find words in the extracts which have the same meaning as a–h below.

Extract A: a decisive issue ……………   b personal involvement ……………
Extract B: c lack of proper food ……………   d go forward ……………
Extract C: e prompt/stimulus ……………   f thoroughly ……………
Extract D: g indirect results ……………   h warnings ……………

16 Unit 3

Genetically modified food

Four writers comment on the advantages and disadvantages of genetically modified food.

A Sonal Panse

Genetically modified organisms (GMO) include crops, vegetables and fruit that have been created using genetic engineering methods. Scientists combine desirable genes from various species to create new genetically-altered crosses with enhanced nutritional, productive and ecological value. This differs from traditional breeding in that genetic transference between unrelated species does not occur biologically in nature. The process of combining inter-species genes does not have the checks and balances that are imposed by nature in traditional breeding. Because of this there is a risk of genetic instability. This means that no one can make any accurate predictions about the long-term effects of GMOs on human beings and the environment. Extensive testing in this regard is either very expensive or impractical, and there is still a great deal about the process that scientists do not understand. This is the crux of the matter in the ongoing debate of GMOs. Food is an emotional topic. It matters greatly to all of us. The subject is also of vested interest for the corporations that manufacture genetically modified seeds and agricultural technologies.

B Deborah Whitman

Genetically-modified foods have the potential to solve many of the world's hunger and malnutrition problems, and to help protect and preserve the environment by increasing yield and reducing reliance upon chemical pesticides and herbicides. Yet there are many challenges ahead for governments, especially in the areas of safety testing, regulation, international policy and food labelling. Many people feel that genetic engineering is an inevitable future development and that we cannot afford to ignore a technology which has such enormous potential benefits. However, we must proceed with caution to avoid causing unintended harm to human health and the environment as a result of our enthusiasm for this powerful technology.

C Deepash Patel

The mere mention of GM foods is a cue for an argument. The benefits of investing large amounts into their research initially appears enticing as they may well provide the answer to combating many of the major issues currently concerning our civilisation. Nevertheless, we must exercise discretion over their use as they may turn out to cause more problems than they solve. The arguments both for and against their development can indeed be convincing but it must be borne in mind that some of these arguments are dictated by economic gain for those organisations involved in the production of these food stuffs. Unless we meticulously make use of the results of their development, the fact that we are going against nature may mean that we are entering this strange new scientific world at our peril. This is a subject which is of the utmost significance to all those who live on earth.

D Afna Sikaala

The fact that not even scientists fully understand the technology or implications of what is involved in GM foods does not seem to prevent people having their own views on the subject. There are those who view their development as the answer to the future of the world, and those who see it as a herald to the end of civilisation as we know it. People have always been sceptical about scientific advances that might affect the world and its inhabitants, but as human beings we cannot stand still. If we had not had the courage of our convictions to press ahead with what we thought to be improvements to our society, we would have made no progress at all over the centuries. True, there may be downsides and caveats to this process which at first sight seem to go against nature, but we should go ahead, confident that the advantages must surely outweigh any problems these GM foods may ultimately create.

Vocabulary

Two-part phrasal verbs

1 Write nouns for phrasal verbs a–d and match them with meanings 1–5 below.

Example

burst out   outburst 3

a cut back   ....
b fall down   ....
c bring up   ....
d put in   ....

1 failure of something or someone
2 raising a child
3 a passing moment of anger
4 reduction in the amount of something
5 effort given to a project, etc.

2 Match the two-part phrasal verbs a–f with meanings 1–6.

a hand out   1 understand
b make out   2 distribute
c knock out   3 lose consciousness
d stand out   4 produce or make
e turn out   5 be noticeable
f pass out   6 eliminate in a competition

3 Use the correct form of the phrasal verbs from 2 to complete these sentences.

a .... leaflets in the High Street has to be one of the most boring jobs!
b There's no doubt that wearing designer clothes makes you .... in a crowd.
c How can Tim be a medical student when he .... as soon as he sees blood?
d Nobody can .... what her motives were in telling so many lies.
e Unfortunately the basketball team got .... in the first round of the tournament.
f This factory is our most productive – it .... an amazing 1,000 cars a week.

4 Look up each of the verbs in bold (in a–f) below to find the correct particle to complete the sentences. Then match them with meanings 1–6.

a The armed robber told the cashier to **hand** *in/on/over* the money in the till.
b What do you **make** *of/up/to* this letter from my ex-boyfriend? I'm not sure how to interpret it.
c Our elderly neighbour **passed** *off/away/up* last week so the family are selling his house.
d The manager is unable to speak at the conference tomorrow so I'm going to **stand** *in/up/to* for him and talk to the delegates.
e I was prepared to lend my brother some money but he **turned** *back/over/down* my offer.
f Two people were **knocked** *away/off/down* by a car on a pedestrian crossing this morning.

1 take someone's place
2 give (not voluntarily)
3 hit and cause to fall
4 die
5 reject
6 understand by

18 Unit 3

Grammar Future forms

1 Read the text about an unusual play and use the correct future form of the verbs below to complete gaps 1–8.

> sell out   know   find out   talk   meet
> perform   not affect   give

> Mike Leigh is a playwright who works without a script, so the actors have to improvise. For this reason, his new play does not even have a title. But by next Friday morning, Leigh 1 .... whether his new play 2 .... with the approval of the critics or not. On Thursday evening, the cast 3 .... 'A New Play by Mike Leigh' for the first time and before an audience who 4 .... virtually nothing about it.
>
> The fact that this is his first play for 12 years is unlikely to be a problem and 5 .... its performance at the box office. Theatregoers expect that tickets for the play's first run of performances 6 .... long before the first night, when it is hoped the play 7 .... a title. One thing, however, is certain – whatever the play is about, Leigh fans 8 .... about it for many weeks to come.

2 Which of the expressions in a–f is followed by the constructions in 1 and 2?
1 the infinitive with *to*
2 *of + ing*

a   just about
b   bound
c   on the point
d   certain
e   no possibility whatsoever
f   no chance

3 Use some of the expressions in 2 to describe your plans for the year ahead – starting from now!

Grammar Extra

Adjective and adverb order

4 The categories below show adjective order before a noun. Put the adjectives into the correct place.

> china   orange   Russian   young   rectangular
> ancient   oval   purple   Chinese   silk
> fascinating   tiny   disgusting   heavy

your opinion   ....
size/weight   ....
age   ....
shape   ....
colour   ....
country of origin   ....
material   ....

5 Answer questions a–d about adverbs.

a   What is the correct order for the adverbial phrases of place and manner in this sentence?
The Prime Minister spoke.
(at the conference/very well)
Where could you add *on Saturday*?

b   Where would you normally put the adverb *probably* in these sentences?
Christopher knows the way to our house.
Jill doesn't know the way.

c   Which emphasising adverb would you use in these sentences?
I quite/just agree with you.
I quite/just love your new flat.

d   Where would you put the adverbs *very* or *pretty* in this sentence?
I can see the ship clearly on the horizon now.

Unit 3

Listening Part 3 Multiple choice

1 Look at the photos of Sally and Pete Fletcher planning a trip across Siberia on motorbikes. What difficulties do you think they may face?

2 🎧 Listen to an interview with the couple, and for questions 1–6, choose the answer (A, B, C or D) which fits best.

1 Pete says their forthcoming trip will challenge them because of the
 A kind of terrain they are crossing.
 B enormous distances they are covering.
 C means of transport they are using.
 D length of time they are taking.

2 Sally says she and Pete were motivated to go on the trip because of a
 A need for excitement.
 B lifelong ambition.
 C desire to earn money.
 D plan to write a book.

3 How does Pete feel about tackling the journey?
 A He thinks that their chances of succeeding are above average.
 B He would prefer not to talk about what might happen.
 C He's excited about the dangers they're about to experience.
 D He suspects they're about to face their toughest challenge yet.

4 According to Sally, how have friends and family reacted to their journey?
 A They have offered them their help if it should be needed.
 B They have expressed their doubts about the success of the venture.
 C They have advised them which route to take across Siberia.
 D They have encouraged them to carry on and not be dispirited.

5 They are going to ensure their safety and well-being during the journey by
 A carrying enough supplies for the whole trip.
 B avoiding routes which are known to be dangerous.
 C making sure they have enough hot meals.
 D wearing suitable clothing for the climate.

6 What comment does Sally make about the weather during their journey?
 A Unexpected bad weather often interferes with timings for stops.
 B Whatever the weather, they will try to stick to the scheduled stop times.
 C If the weather is against them, they will be forced to abandon their trip.
 D Bad weather has less effect on motorbikes than other forms of transport.

20 Unit 3

Use of English Part 1 Multiple-choice cloze

1 Read the text below, ignoring the gaps, to find out why the 'body clock' is important.

2 For questions 1–8, read the text again and decide which answer (A, B, C or D) best fits each gap.
Example
0 B

A FUTURE IN THE DARK

Many of us are working, travelling and shopping in hours that used to be (0) ...B... for relaxation and sleep. But, according to scientists, we are no longer getting enough darkness in our lives. In fact, (1) .... shows that a growing number of health and environmental problems are (2) .... to a loss of darkness.

Life has evolved with a day/night cycle – without this, people experience an adverse impact on their immume systems. We are (3) .... a conflict between what our mind wants, and what our internal body clock prepares us for. This biological clock is similar to the conductor of an orchestra, with the multiple rhythms of the body (4) .... the orchestra sections.

The body clock is (5) .... on the light/dark cycle and ensures that all our internal systems – temperature, alertness, blood pressure and so on – are working together. This is its sole (6) .... By moving to 24-hour living, and not taking into (7) .... darkness, we are effectively throwing away the advantages of evolution, (8) .... we admit it or not.

0	A conserved	B reserved	C upheld	D defended
1	A demonstration	B display	C research	D confirmation
2	A prone	B open	C due	D next
3	A creating	B contributing	C giving	D increasing
4	A describing	B corresponding	C expressing	D representing
5	A done	B based	C decided	D established
6	A reason	B project	C purpose	D desire
7	A interest	B importance	C detail	D account
8	A so that	B whether	C unless	D in case

Unit 3   21

Review Units 1-3

1 Read definitions a–g, then complete the compound nouns.

a   a place where things are made or repaired
    = work...............
b   a problem which makes a situation worse
    = set...............
c   an important development in a situation
    = break...............
d   someone who sells papers and magazines
    = news...............
e   the written text of a movie
    = film...............
f   an unexpected result of a situation or action
    = side...............
g   the number of people attending an event
    = turn...............

2 Complete the phrasal verbs in a–f with a suitable verb in the correct form.

a   What makes Jim .... out in a crowd is his long, dark hair.
b   Unfortunately, our request for a loan was .... down by the bank.
c   It's a pity the baseball team was .... out of the championship last night.
d   We'll have to make an effort to .... back on our expenditure this month.
e   Do you think that children who are .... up in the countryside have a happier childhood?
f   You need to .... up for yourself when talking to Jim. He's a bully!

3 Correct the mistakes in adjective and adverb order.

a   Tim had a rather small extremely fascinating group of friends.
b   Did you at the beach enjoy yourself yesterday?
c   We found the pretty restaurant easily.
d   What a table disgusting oval wooden old!
e   I love just your new dress.
f   What a rectangular dirty enormous pencil case!
g   Brenda likes quite being on her own.

4 Put the words in the correct order beginning with the words in bold.

a   photograph John **I** showed the.
b   her for bicycle brother a bought birthday **Susie** his.
c   me a fortune **My** new car cost!
d   seeing Robert's insisted **The authorities** visa on.
e   coffee the **Fetch** you would visitors some?
f   extra the holiday students an promised day's **The** principal.
g   having wisdom **My** dentist recommended teeth taken out two.
h   it to careful leave appliance the switched not on after **Be** using.

5 Complete the adjectives in sentences a–e.

a   Good teachers are sens............... to the needs of their students.
b   After an exhaust............... international trip, the President will take a break this summer.
c   Children love stories and imagin............... heroes.
d   One of the most satisf............... things about sport is that it helps people develop team skills.
e   Fortunately, our members of staff are all consci............... and hard-working.

6 Rewrite the second sentence in a–c keeping the meaning the same. Use three to six words including the word given.

a   We think it would be better for the guests to arrive much earlier.
    PREFER
    We ....
    the guests arrived much earlier.
b   The football team managed to win the trophy for a second year.
    SUCCEEDED
    The football team ....
    the trophy for a second year.
c   Please note that our advice would be to wash the appliance before using it.
    RECOMMEND
    Please note that ....
    the appliance before using it.

22   Review Units 1–3

7 Complete sentences a–e using one of the nouns below.

> upbringing   cutbacks   downfall   input   outburst

a As a member of the student union, we would very much like your …………… on this matter.
b She is normally a very calm, relaxed person. I don't know where that sudden …………… came from.
c The scandal surrounding the politician brought about his …………… .
d I regret to say that due to the …………… , we will be unable to afford our annual party this year.
e What do you think has the greatest influence on your life, your …………… or your education?

8 Complete sentences a–e using a suitable expression with *get*.

a These endless discussions are getting us …………… . It's time we reached an agreement.
b You should meet my sister. You'd get …………… really well with her.
c Let's get …………… to business. What's the first item on the agenda?
d As it's getting …………… for 7 p.m., I think we should draw the session to a close.
e We can't get …………… of going to the party without offending someone.

9 Complete a–f with a relative pronoun and, where necessary, a preposition. More than one answer may be possible.

a This is the place …………… the accident occurred.
b Africa, …………… culture is extremely diverse, is a huge continent.
c The poet, …………… very little is known, lived in the north of Scotland.
d It would be interesting to know …………… Thomas decided to leave the football club.
e There was a time …………… deer roamed wild through these woods.
f Debbie has painted numerous landscapes, some …………… are on display in the exhibition.

10 Choose the best adjective to complete sentences 1–7.

1 The teaching staff were …………… in their intention to improve examination results.
  a depressed   b resolute   c curious
2 Despite the disappointing sales figures, we are …………… about the future of the company.
  a realistic   b curious   c optimistic
3 I now feel …………… that I can make myself understood when I'm speaking Italian.
  a cheerful   b depressed   c confident
4 It is hardly …………… to expect to fulfil all our dreams and ambitions in life.
  a realistic   b pessimistic   c optimistic
5 Everyone is …………… with Sarah's moody behaviour.
  a fed up   b depressed   c pessimistic
6 The new ballet is a very …………… interpretation of a traditional, classic theme.
  a conscientious   b imaginative   c sensible
7 Your work is …………… but it could be so much better.
  a satisfactory   b depressing   c sensitive

11 Use future expressions to write sentences about the likelihood of the following happening.

Example
the world's population increasing
The population of the world is bound to increase, because …

a humans living on Mars
…………………………………………………………
b the cost of public transport rising
…………………………………………………………
c robots becoming part of our daily life
…………………………………………………………
d the whole world speaking the same language
…………………………………………………………
e your country's football team winning the world cup
…………………………………………………………
f everyone in your class passing the exam
…………………………………………………………

Review Units 1–3

Into the wild 4

Reading Part 7 Gapped text

1 Read the article, and paragraphs A–G, about learning to dive, and find out what words a–c refer to.
  a double-decker bus   b swimming pool   c 'buddy'

2 Read the article again and choose from the paragraphs A–G the one which fits each gap (1–6). There is one extra paragraph which you do not need to use.

take the plunge

My friend and I were on holiday in the Dominican Republic when our hotel offered us a trial scuba dive. You could just put on the equipment in the swimming pool and try it. My friend wasn't remotely
5 interested in going scuba-diving, but I gave it a go.

1..
Each piece looked intimidating and I was alarmed at suddenly being responsible for the air we breathe. But in reality, it's similar to driving a car. You have an air gauge for your tank, which you watch like the
10 fuel supply, and a depth gauge that's like reading the speedometer. After a while, everything becomes second nature.

2..
Suddenly, I'd discovered this completely silent world. I'm a make-up artist; it's an industry where everyone
15 is always chatting. Although there were people around during the dive, the experience was entirely my own. I'd wanted to try a calming therapy like yoga for ages, but never got round to it. Here, I had to keep my breathing steady and before I knew it, I
20 was completely relaxed, lost in beautiful colours and a myriad of sea creatures.

3..
I realised I wanted to take up this new hobby seriously. So, back in England I started an Introduction to Diving Skills course. Going from the
25 Dominican Republic to my local pool fortunately wasn't as bad as I'd expected.

4..
I knew that your emergency air supply is actually with your dive partner and how the thing you must not do is to hold your breath, because you risk
30 bursting a lung.
You should also swot up on where you want to go diving. I really enjoyed history when I was at school, so I love wreck-diving to see it all come to life. Diving lets you see things, in their natural surroundings,
35 which no one has seen before.

5..
Our breaks away triggered my decision to teach scuba-diving. And having done the introduction course, I realised it was important to learn slowly and thoroughly – on holiday I saw people in the water
40 who didn't have a clue about the dangers of coming up too quickly, being too long underwater, or not watching their air. I wanted to become a better diver myself and to help others dive safely.

6..
I teach once a month now at one of the top dive
45 centres in the UK. It's so rewarding, especially when you are with someone who's done their first dive and just discovered an exciting new world without boundaries.

24 Unit 4

A

It was wonderful to go below the surface and to spend time just observing and moving along weightlessly. I saw a turtle on that first dive. It left me completely in awe, even though it totally ignored me.

B

To become a competent diver, he recommended the following steps. First, take an introductory course. Next, do the five theory modules, which end with a test. But he also pointed out that to qualify to dive with a 'buddy' of the same qualification or higher, you need to complete a further four supervised dives, this time in open water.

C

As well as opening up this forgotten world, it brought me into contact with my partner, Roger. I met him on a training excursion to a double-decker bus that had been deliberately sunk. My friend had an ear problem so Roger offered to partner me. We went on countless dives together and now we go on diving holidays too.

D

The very first session was extremely short but, surprisingly, it was enough time to get to grips with the equipment. There was a mask and some fins, a snorkel-like mouthpiece which you breathe through and a buoyancy control device which you inflate or deflate depending on how deep you wanted to dive.

E

That first time you go out on your own with someone who's totally dependent on you, it's terrifying. I used to be overly cautious – if they were even slightly worried, I took them straight back to the top. But I've learned lots of ways to help people relax underwater.

F

That 20-minute session was followed by a dive in the sea. After that, I was hooked. Other than being shown how to put everything on, there was no further training; not something I'd recommend now. I was taken ten metres down and, despite being followed by a guide, I had the most wonderful feeling of freedom.

G

The real shock came four months later when I did an open water dive at a place called Grangewaters. When I went in, the water temperature was only about four degrees. It's full of black mud, so you can't see anything at all. By then I had a very thorough grounding in everything that could go wrong.

Vocabulary
Word formation

1 Write adjective forms of these words in the correct column. You may need to change the spelling. Can you think of other adjectives with these endings? Try to add one to each column.

> malice control force argument memory
> outrage possibility inform submission
> mystery suspicion terror advantage

-ive	-ious	-eous	-able	-ible

2 Use adjectives from 1 to replace the words in italics in sentences a–i.

a After the game, the police struggled to deal with the *scandalous* behaviour of the football supporters.
b Bella's a great friend but she does tend to be *quarrelsome* at times.
c The discovery of a *dangerous-looking* package resulted in the closure of the railway station.
d It may have been *educational* but the presentation was also extremely tedious!
e Richard is so *uncomplaining and unquestioning*. He should learn to stand up for himself more.
f Don't listen to a word Janet says – it's all *spiteful* gossip.
g William's *strange* disappearance led to a police search of the area where he lived.
h I think it would be *extremely useful* to get some work experience to help your job application.
i What is the most *unforgettable* holiday you've had? For me, it's travelling around New Zealand.

3 Look up nouns a–d below (from 1) in a dictionary and answer questions 1–3 for each one.

a submission
b argument
c memory
d terror

1 Is the verb form above or below the noun entry?
2 What other words appear to derive from the noun?
3 Can you find any new expressions or collocations?

> **tip**
> Scanning through an entry in a dictionary will help you understand word formation.

26 Unit 4

Grammar

Past tenses

1 Complete the leaflet by putting the verbs in brackets into the correct form of the present perfect or the past perfect.

HELP SAVE THE ORANG-UTAN
DID YOU KNOW THAT ?

- humans **1** .... (*cut*) down their habitat for years.
- land which **2** .... (*previously/cover*) with vegetation was cleared for mining and plantation.
- the orang-utan **3** .... (*now/lose*) 80% of its natural habitat.
- many **4** .... (*kill*) by farmers who believed orang-utans **5** .... (*become*) a pest.
- it **6** .... (*recently/add*) on the endangered list – fewer than 40,000 now exist.

Last year a campaign was set up for people who **7** .... (*never/show*) active interest in conservation to help save the orang-utan.

Grammar Extra

Articles

2 Underline the correct use of the article in each pair of sentences in 1–7.

1. a Some marketing experience is desirable to run (a, no article) **business** successfully.
   b Our local cinema is back in (the, no article) **business** after its refurbishment.
2. a (The, no article) idle **gossip** can often have unexpected consequences.
   b Polly is (a, no article) **well-known gossip**, so don't tell her anything.
3. a (A, no article) previous **experience** is essential for this job.
   b The book outlines all (the, no article) **experiences** the writer had in Africa.
4. a (An, no article) **interest** in the museum's latest exhibition has been tremendous.
   b (An, no article) **interest** is payable on this account but it is so low it is not worth having.
5. a (A, The) **country** is undoubtedly a far healthier place to live than the town.
   b (A, no article) **country** which attracts many foreign visitors is Thailand.
6. a This new restaurant definitely has a touch of (the, no article) **class**.
   b (A, no article) **class** of 35 students is almost impossible to teach effectively.
7. a Due to increased security (a, no article) **people** have to put up with long delays at airports.
   b The President urged (a, the) **people** to turn out in force and vote in the referendum.

3 Complete gaps 1–12 with *a*, *an*, *the* or no article.

Every month we're giving away 1 .... magical holiday. Don't miss this unique opportunity to sample 2 .... luxury of our Transglobe holidays in one of 3 .... world's most sought-after destinations: 4 .... Pacific. Or perhaps you have a secret passion to travel to 5 .... destinations such as Venice, experience 6 .... exciting adventure in 7 .... sports car, or learn to cook 8 .... Eastern delicacies in 9 .... Orient? Just log on to our travel service website and, if you don't win, you can find 10 .... latest destinations and advice on how to plan a trip. At 11 .... end of each holiday, we'll give you 12 .... vouchers to be used towards your next holiday with us.

Unit 4

Listening Part 2 Sentence completion

1 Look at the photos. What athletic abilities do you think these animals have?

2 🎧 You will hear part of a radio programme about the athleticism of animals. For questions 1–8, complete the sentences.

ANIMAL ATHLETES

One small ant can lift (1) .... times its own body weight.

Ants have an amazingly large number of (2) ....

It takes the cheetah just (3) .... seconds to cover a distance of 100m.

Cheetahs can reach high speeds, thanks to their enlarged internal organs and their (4) ....

The cheetah, however, has a low (5) ....

Springbok are frequently seen jumping in the (6) .... season.

Archer fish catch (7) .... with a 1.5 metre water jet.

The archer fish carry out their shooting in (8) ....

28 Unit 4

Use of English Part 2 Open cloze

1 Read the text about whale-watching, ignoring the gaps, and find out where the writer went and for how long.

2 For questions 1–8, read the text again and think of the word which best fits each gap.

A SUMMER AT SEA

Spending a summer whale watching off the coast of Patagonia is a (0) ...*once*.... in a lifetime opportunity. We spent twelve hours on the boat every day and learned a great (1) .... about the whales' behaviour.

Generally, we simply had to move a short distance from the coast, switch off the engine and wait. Younger whales were protectively pushed (2) .... by their mothers, but older ones were allowed to play nearby, some even coming close (3) .... for us to touch them.

Often the sea seemed full of whales but at other times we saw (4) .... any at all. Sometimes we could go for days and (5) .... see a single whale.

One day we came upon a whale and her baby. At (6) .... the mother would not let the baby approach us during our visits but, as time (7) .... by, she allowed him to come closer. It was truly amazing to be rewarded (8) .... such trust at the end of our six weeks.

3 Complete sentences a–h with one word.

a Spending a summer in the company of whales is a ....-off experience.
b I'm afraid I know relatively .... about the behaviour of whales.
c The animals will only appear if you wait .... enough.
d Sometimes we saw many whales but .... other occasions, we saw none.
e Some of the whales were .... far away for me to see them clearly.
f Initially, the mother prevented her baby .... approaching the boat.
g It's wonderful that the whales began to .... their trust in us.
h The truth .... that no one really knows exactly how the whales communicate.

Health matters

Reading Part 5 Multiple choice

1 Read the text about human athletic abilities and find out what happened in

   a 1954.
   b 1968.
   c 1991.
   d the 1980s.

2 For questions 1–6, read the text again and choose the answer (A, B, C or D) which you think best fits according to the text.

1 What initial comment does Dr. Jack Wilmore make?
   A There will always be limits to what the human body can achieve.
   B It will become more and more difficult for athletes to break records.
   C Athletics will become one of the most popular forms of exercise.
   D Athletes will continue to surprise us with what they can achieve.

2 The writer mentions athletes like Bannister and Beamon in order to
   A demonstrate the effect their determination to win had on them.
   B prove that even their amazing achievements can be bettered.
   C exemplify what athletes can achieve under stressful conditions.
   D demonstrate how accurately we can measure what athletes are capable of.

3 Dr. Wilmore feels that attitudes within athletics are changing because
   A coaches have begun to realise the importance of more intensive training.
   B experts have begun to highlight the need for more unusual workouts.
   C athletes are now being given mental as well as physical training by experts.
   D coaches now encourage athletes to unwind between training sessions.

4 According to Dr. Wilmore, how are today's children different from years ago?
   A They participate in far more sports.
   B They begin sports at a much earlier age.
   C They become more proficient in their chosen sports.
   D They are more likely to become professional athletes.

5 Dr. Wilmore believes that women
   A have physically developed and advanced over the years.
   B perform equally well whether they are tall or short.
   C now have the same chance as boys of realising their potential.
   D are beginning to play sports at a much younger age than boys.

6 What conclusion does Dr. Wilmore make?
   A We try to push the human body to its limits at our peril.
   B We must congratulate ourselves on what athletes have achieved so far.
   C We need to do more research into what the human body is capable of.
   D We should not prejudge what might be beyond our physical capabilities.

Unit 5

Limits of the human body

In the second millennium, one frequently asked question is: What are the limits of the human body? Is there a point at which we human beings might consider that it is physically impossible to do something? We decided to consult the experts to find out.

'One thing we've all learned in the last 30 years or so is that just about anything is humanly possible,' says Dr. Jack Wilmore, from Texas A&M University and author of *The Physiology of Sport and Exercise*, part of which examines the limits of the human body.

'As the new millennium progresses, I think you'll see more records continue to fall in every sport. The talent pool is better than ever. Never before have so many good athletes competed, and not just in this country, but all over the world. With more people involved and competing, records will fall and new standards will be set.'

Many believed it was physically impossible for a human to run a mile in under four minutes, but Roger Bannister proved that theory wrong with a three minute, 59 second mile (1.609 kilometres) in 1954. Today, sub four-minute miles are considered not to be the extraordinary achievements they were deemed to be in the 1950s but mere routine, even in high school. In addition to this, Bob Beamon stretched human performance in the 1968 Olympics with his historic long jump of 8.9027 metres. In an event in which a record is usually broken by mere inches, he shattered the previous jump by 0.6096 metres, but even his record was broken in 1991.

'We've all seen reports of people doing superhuman feats of strength under duress, such as a man lifting a car off a child,' Wilmore adds. 'So we know that the human body can do things that go far beyond normal activity. That's why it's foolish to say any record can't be broken. Who's to say it won't happen?'

The reasons for this astonishing change in the ability of human beings to achieve bigger and better results from improved stamina are many and varied, as well as being somewhat controversial. Are we simply growing stronger and becoming healthier, or is there a more complicated explanation for what seems to be happening to the human race? One additional factor which is just now becoming more understood and heavily emphasised is known as sports psychology. What it seems to prove is that getting inside the athlete's head can be as effective as training and long workouts, which in the past were considered to be the only way of improving performance and pushing the human body to its limits.

According to Wilmore, the psychological aspect of sports should not be ignored or discounted because we now know that it is what makes the athlete tick mentally that can be all-important. He points out that 'most professional teams have hired sports psychologists for their players. It's just another way of tapping into a human's full potential.'

'In addition, every aspect of athletics – training, nutrition, injury treatment – is far better than it's ever been. Better coaching, training techniques, equipment and other factors all contribute to make today's athlete more competitive than ever,' he believes. 'Children today tend to specialize in one or two sports instead of competing in several as was common twenty-five years ago,' Wilmore says. 'That means they start concentrating on a sport much earlier and more intensely, and they become much better at it.'

But what about the difference between the performance of men and that of women? Is there any reason why men should be expected to perform better or is it possible for both sexes to achieve the same results? Wilmore says that the chances of women achieving new heights in athletics could be greater than men, as more women are now involved in sports than at any other time and they are starting at about the same age as boys, meaning they are more skilled than the previous generation of girls. 'Plus, women are taller and stronger than ever. It used to be rare to see a girl who towered above you. Now it seems like you see them every day.'

'There's a lot we don't know yet about the human body,' he adds. 'And one of those things is the full range of human potential. It can be foolish to try and put limits on what the human body can do.'

Who knows to what extent humans might yet improve upon their already staggering achievements?

Vocabulary

The body

1 Circle the word in italics to complete the expressions in a–h.

a Could you *give* Sally *a hand/foot/arm* with sorting out the filing system tomorrow?
b We're going out to dinner with the Browns tonight. I suppose we'll have to *hand/finger/foot the bill* as usual.
c Initially, it can be difficult to *get* your *head/brain/mind round* advanced economics.
d What's the name of that hotel we stayed in last year? It's *on the point/end/tip of my tongue*.
e Bob really *put his toes/foot/ankle in it* when he moaned about his boss to Julia. She is his niece!
f It's far too wet to go for a walk. Why don't we *shoulder/arm/head for* that café instead?
g Rob's just bought a hand-made Italian suit but it *cost an arm and a leg/hand/finger*.
h I'm fed up with *working my fingers/hands/wrists to the bone*. It's time I found a job with shorter hours or a better salary.

2 Complete these sentences using suitable expressions from 1.

a When we missed the bus, we decided to .... the taxi rank instead.
b Do you remember the name of that island we visited a few years ago? It's ....
c Jake's a bright student but he just can't seem to .... maths at all.
d Does it really .... to fly to Australia?
e Can anyone .... lifting these boxes? They are so heavy.
f Just for once, can you try not to .... by saying the wrong thing to Aunty Mary?
g I'm certainly not going to .... for you to have another free holiday with your friends!
h I've been .... recently – I'm trying to meet a tight deadline!

Word formation

3 Use a dictionary to help you fill in the nouns in the table below. More than one answer might be possible.

Verb	Noun (person)	Noun (thing)
a survive		
b perform		
c terrorise		
d coordinate		
e immigrate		
f defend		
g coach		
h achieve		

4 Use the correct form of the words from 3 to complete sentences a–h.

a Afternoon .... of the play begin at 2.30. Latecomers will not be admitted.
b .... to the USA must complete all appropriate forms before entering the country.
c The government has brought in strict new legislation to combat the threat of ....
d Throughout her life, Maria was a strong and active .... of women's rights.
e After the fire on the ocean-liner, ... were picked up by a passing cargo ship.
f To be a top tennis player, you need to have excellent hand-eye ....
g Amongst his many .... , the President managed to maintain economic stability.
h Rail passengers will be transferred to waiting .... to complete the rest of their journey by road.

5 Look up *compete* in a dictionary. Scan through the words that derive from it to find:

a words that collocate with the noun (person and thing) forms.
b the different meanings of the adjective form.

Unit 5

Grammar

Direct speech

1 Read an interview with a famous explorer, Alan Bent. Then rewrite what he said into indirect speech using the verbs in brackets at the end of sentences 1–8.

Example
I met up with famous explorer Alan Bent and asked him how difficult it is to be an explorer. He said …

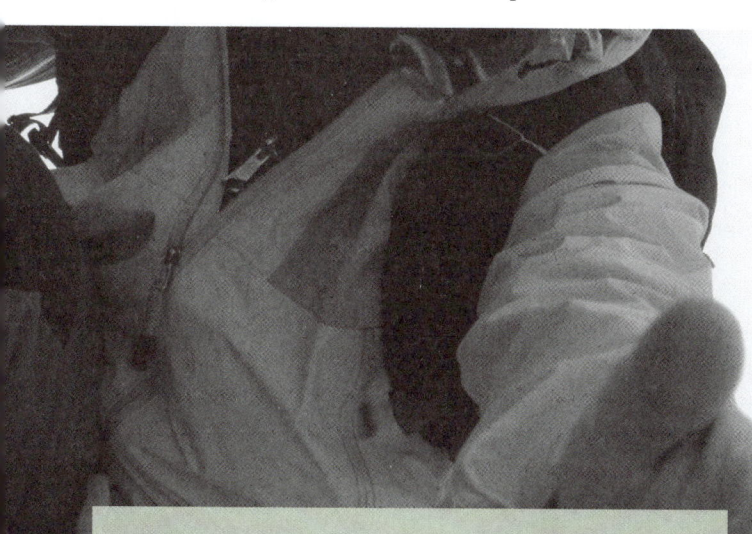

'It means I have to try to keep myself in good physical shape (1 say). Travelling to remote places means long periods away from the things most people take for granted, such as doctors (2 tell). I always wear my boots in bed (3 admit). You see, I'm very tall so my feet always stick out of the bed (4 explain). And someone in my hut was bitten by a snake once (5 add)! Oh, and I always carry an emergency medical kit, which contains a needle and thread (6 go on to say). Why don't you join me on one of these expeditions to see what it's like (7 suggest)? But make sure you keep your boots on at night (8 warn)!'

Grammar Extra

Prefixes

2 Underline the word in each group which <u>cannot</u> be used with prefixes a–g.

a un   reasonable/steady/productive/considerate
b in   natural/comprehensible/competent/credible
c im   mature/correct/precise/practical
d dis organised/compatible/connected/honest
e mis treated/understood/known/pronounced
f non- suitable/violent/fiction/existent
g il   flammable/legal/legible/logical

3 Complete sentences a–i with a word from 2.

a A .... protest against tougher laws for asylum-seekers on university fees took place in the city yesterday.
b I fear the plans for dealing with traffic congestion might turn out to be rather ....
c While most members of the staff are extremely good at their job, one or two are rather ....
d We don't have a phone any longer – the line was .... by the phone company.
e The writing on this prescription is completely .... I can't make out a single word.
f Unwanted pets can often be neglected or even .... by their owners.
g Bill has been rather .... on his feet since he fell off his bike.
h What you are asking me to do is totally .... ! It wouldn't be fair to expect anyone to do something as difficult as this.
i I don't read many novels. I prefer reading ....

Unit 5

Listening

Part 1 Multiple choice

1 Think of five ways schools or parents can encourage children to adopt healthier lifestyles.

2 🎧 Read questions 1–6 below before you listen to the three different extracts. Then listen and choose the answer (A, B or C) which fits best.

extract one
You hear part of an interview with an actress called Mary Taylor Ward.

1 Why did Mary release her fitness video?
   A Many famous people had also done this.
   B It would help her lose weight.
   C She had a lot of relevant experience.

2 She wanted people to watch the video in order to
   A challenge their own fitness goals.
   B have a good time while exercising.
   C learn about another side of her life.

extract two
You hear part of an interview with a health expert talking about what to do at lunchtimes.

3 Why does the expert suggest a walk at lunchtimes?
   A to benefit from air and sunshine
   B to develop an appetite for lunch
   C to aid recovery from health problems

4 What does the expert advise people to do in bad weather?
   A Read interesting magazines or books.
   B Take part in indoor exercise.
   C Do puzzles or something similar.

extract three
You hear two people on a radio programme talking about a recent campaign for healthy school dinners.

5 What do the speakers agree about?
   A Cafeterias are more busy.
   B Children should eat healthily.
   C Other menus should be considered.

6 The man thinks that the campaign failed because
   A the change was too sudden.
   B school cooks had to be retrained.
   C children naturally want to eat junk food.

Use of English

Part 3 Word formation

1 Read the text below quickly and decide which summary, a or b, is the most suitable.

a A short workout is better than no workout.
b A short workout is better than a long workout.

2 For questions 1–8, read the text again and use the words given in capitals to form a word for each gap.

A quick workout

For those with (0) ...insufficient... time to work out in the gym, there is some good news. Fitness enthusiasts can effectively reduce their workout time by two-thirds, according to recent research. Gym (1) .... has soared in recent years, and doctors are hoping that these (2) .... will encourage more people to take up exercise.

The results suggest that it is not (3) .... to spend hours exercising when working out for a shorter time and more (4) .... achieves the same results. Participants were required to cut their exercise time but increase the difficulty of their workout. Those who exercised for the shorter time found that a significant (5) .... in body fat had occured. Experts believe that this proves that a streamlined exercise programme is more (6) .... and less time-consuming.

Some (7) .... point out, however, that to achieve goals like these, you need a good level of fitness before tackling exercise of such (8) ....

0	SUFFICE	5	REDUCE
1	MEMBER	6	BENEFIT
2	FIND	7	CRITICISE
3	PRODUCE	8	INTENSE
4	ENERGY		

3 Fill in the missing parts of speech in the table below.

	Verb	Noun	Adjective	Adverb
a	enthuse	....	....	....
b	reduce	....		
c	encourage	....		
d	achieve	....		
e	increase			....
f	signify	....	....	....
g	occur	....		
h	criticise	....	....	....

4 Write the words in brackets in the correct form in a–c.
a Wait until you've heard both sides of the .... (argue) before making a .... (judge).
b Today's front page story contains .... (drama) .... (reveal) about the travel industry.
c The storyline is very .... (romance) and the book is .... (exception) well written.

5 Look up the words <u>not</u> used in 4 in a dictionary. Write sentences to show at least two different meanings or uses of the words.

Unit 5

Would you believe it?

Reading

Part 8 Multiple matching

1 Read the text about superheroes. How does the writer ultimately feel about the characters in the films?

- inspired
- disappointed
- angry

2 In which section (A–F) of the text are 1–10 mentioned? The sections may be chosen more than once.

an assault on an innocent person	1 …	2 …
a seemingly endless collection of costumes	3 …	
a box-office hit for superheroes	4 …	
a heroine frightened of beginning relationships with men	5 …	
a summary of the drawbacks of being a superhero	6 …	7 …
a secret and harmful invention that is uncovered	8 …	
a heroine who seems to detest herself	9 …	
a search for something which causes global suffering	10 …	

CAN GIRLS BE SUPERHEROES?

A

Batman is still high up in the charts, having earned $200m. Superman is back. We are held hostage by larger-than-life male superheroes. If little
5 boys have these figures, who can little girls admire? I head off in search of an inspirational female superhero and buy four films young people might have watched over the last few years:
10 *Catwoman, Elektra, Lara Croft Tomb Raider: The Cradle of Life* and *Charlie's Angels: Full Throttle*.

36 Unit 6

B

My first supergirl is Catwoman. Patience Philips, played by Halle Berry, is a graphic designer at a cosmetics company. When Patience discovers that evil genius Laurel Hedare has designed a new face cream to make Americans ugly, Hedare ensures that she meets with a fatal accident. Although Patience dies, she is reanimated by cats. She finds a guru who says, 'Catwomen are not contained by the rules of society. You will often be lonely.' I begin to despair. Catwoman, I decide, is a loser. She finds a cop boyfriend then steals a shopful of jewellery and returns it in a bag marked: 'Sorry'. Surely a supergirl never says sorry? She is also thick. Hedare frames her for murder – easily. Kitty has to sob to be released from jail. My finger trembles over 'Eject'. But perhaps she'll improve. She doesn't. Although she rescues the world from killer face cream, the boyfriend is dumped and Patience pads into the moonlight alone. This is not superheroic, it's a pathetic example of unnecessary self-sacrifice.

C

My next potential idol is Elektra. She is a reincarnated, knife-throwing, ninja babe-assassin who only stabs people when wearing tight red satin. 'Legend tells of a warrior – a lost soul,' says a voice on the film. A pattern is emerging here – a superheroine always has to be lost. Elektra is not only lost, she is, according to mentor Terence Stamp, 'poisoned by tragedy.' Even her protector cannot protect her from the truth. My heart sinks. Elektra is bitter – 'Nobody tells the truth about themselves' – and her dialogue comes from television scripts – 'My mother died when I was young.' Like Catwoman, Elektra is not super enough to have a functioning relationship. When she does kiss a man, she panics. 'I'm not the kind of person to get involved with,' she sobs.

D

Another pattern is emerging. At one point, the villainous Hand breathes on Elektra's face and gives her spots. In Superland, the worse thing you can do to a superwoman is give her acne. Elektra triumphs over Hand, but pays the price. Just two films in, the message to women from Hollywood is: You want to be a superwoman? Are you sure? Well, unhappiness and being miserable are obligatory. Elektra clearly does dislike it and slumps into self-loathing. She stares at a ninja teenager and whines: 'Please don't let her turn out like me.'

E

The girls with supernatural powers were unsuper. So I turn to the women with superskills, beginning with Lara Croft, as played by Angelina Jolie. Lara is like the girls I was at school with: ordinary girls who talk like film actresses and live in large houses in the countryside. Her quest is to find the mythical Pandora's Box, before evil scientists get it. She drives a motorbike along the Great Wall of China and sky-dives, but then 'The Message' pops up again. 'You're afraid of letting anyone in,' says her boyfriend. Lara shoots him, without apparent justification, then becomes a noble superheroine-in-solitude. So, superwoman can't have a super relationship and the pay-off for her super gift is loneliness and misanthropy.

F

My quest for a superwoman ends with Charlie's Angels. The Angels, wearing tight clothes, get rid of a gaggle of cheery gangsters. Then they return to LA, to serve their patriarch Charlie – an elusive man who delivers orders, assists from afar, and congratulates them appropriately – and are informed they must recover some important data for the FBI. They succeed with a combination of looking gorgeous, karate, and disco-dancing. They change their outfits every thirty seconds and wear aquamarine mascara and, after two hours, the Angels see off baddie Demi Moore. It is certainly not heroic. Under their masks, I saw only weakness. Batman has won.

Vocabulary

Truth and lies

1 Choose the best answer (A, B or C) to complete sentences 1–5.

1 The accused tried in vain to .... the true nature of the crime he had committed.
   A conceal   B shelter   C protect
2 We have evidence to prove that the new car was paid for with .... money.
   A copy   B counterfeit   C mock
3 We have complete .... in the government's ability to solve problems of unemployment.
   A loyalty   B honour   C faith
4 Stuart managed to .... everyone in with elaborate stories about his childhood.
   A have   B put   C take
5 You can rely on Elizabeth to give you good advice. I'd .... her judgement every time.
   A trust   B presume   C assume

Words with similar meanings

2 Look up the words in 1–3 in a dictionary. Match one from each pair with definition a, then complete the definitions for b.

1 snigger/giggle
   a laugh in a silly way when amused, embarrassed or nervous
   b laugh in a(n) .... way
2 whisper/mumble
   a speak in a quiet way that is not clear
   b deliberately speak very quietly so ....
3 eavesdrop/overhear
   a hear, especially by accident, a conversation in which you are not involved
   b .... to what other people are saying

3 Complete sentences a–c with words from 2 in the correct form.

a How do you know that? You must have been .... We haven't told anyone!
b All the students .... nervously as they waited for their exam results.
c Try not to .... when you speak. No one can hear you properly.

Meanings of *hold*

4 How many different meanings and uses of *hold* can you think of? Compare your ideas with a dictionary. Which meanings and uses did you not think of?

5 Complete sentences a–f with a suitable word or phrase (1–6).

1 for questioning
2 responsible
3 a party
4 extreme views
5 my attention
6 the line

a Teachers will be *held* .... for the behaviour of pupils in their class.
b Two men were *held* .... in connection with the break-ins.
c I enjoyed the play but it didn't *hold* .... as much as the playwright's last one.
d The election result was surprising as the winning candidate *held* ....
e We're going to *hold* .... next month for our anniversary.
f Can you *hold* .... and I'll put you through to my secretary?

6 Match the different meanings of *hold* from 5 with definitions a–f below.

a wait momentarily
b make liable
c have an event
d kept somewhere and not allowed to leave
e possess or show
f keep someone's interest

Grammar

Modals

1 Circle the most suitable modal in these sentences.

a You *shouldn't/mustn't* have wasted your time typing out the letter. You knew we weren't going to send it.
b A work permit *must/need* be obtained in advance by anyone intending to live and reside in the country.
c You *need/should* always seek advice before signing any legal documentation.
d The staff *must/should* be very contented working here. Everyone has a smile on their face.
e I suppose your order *might/can* have been lost. These things can happen.
f I'm afraid I *can't/shouldn't* make out what the writing on this prescription says – it's illegible.
g You *ought to/need* think carefully before making any decision.

2 Complete these sentences using modals of assumption or deduction and the correct form of one of the verbs below.

   miss   delay   receive   be   pass   do

a She <u>must have passed</u>. the exam – look, she's smiling and laughing!
b The hotel .... our booking as they had no reservation under the name 'Wright'.
c It's odd that James hasn't arrived yet – do you think his plane .... ?
d I think you .... him actually, he's normally gone by this time.
e You .... well at the interview, otherwise they wouldn't have offered you the job!
f Surely Sally .... serious when she said she was going to sell all her possessions and go and live on a desert island?

3 Match the modals in a–c with meanings 1–3.

a Visitors needn't return the museum catalogue – it's theirs to keep.
b Passengers with season tickets don't need to purchase tickets on a daily basis.
c I needn't have called directory enquiries. I had the number in my diary after all.

1 It was done, but it was not necessary.
2 It is not necessary, but can be done (if required).
3 This is not necessary.

4 Complete sentences a–d with *needn't* or *needn't have* and the correct form of the verbs in brackets.

a 'I stayed up late revising, but when I saw the exam paper, I realised I .... (worry)!'
b 'You .... (pay) anything now. A bill will be sent to you in due course.'
c 'Apparently fans .... (arrive) early for the concert – there will be plenty of available seats.'
d 'We .... (spend) all that time looking for a bank – there was a cash machine here!'

Unit 6 39

Listening

Part 4 Multiple matching

1 Do you agree with these comments about food?

- Breakfast is the most important meal of the day.
- Eating carrots helps you see in the dark.
- Eating fish will make you more clever.

2 🎧 Listen to five people talking about popular beliefs connected with food and complete the exam task below.

For 1–5, choose from the list A–H the person who is speaking.

A a teacher
B a nutritionist
C an athlete
D a mother
E a chef
F a doctor's receptionist
G a researcher
H a writer

Speaker 1 [1]
Speaker 2 [2]
Speaker 3 [3]
Speaker 4 [4]
Speaker 5 [5]

For 6–10, choose from the list A–H each speaker's beliefs about a particular food or meal.

A It improves your mental abilities.
B It can cut visits to the doctor.
C It leads to poorer performance if missed.
D It will make you beautiful.
E It can develop physical strength.
F It helps improve one of the senses.
G It is normally avoided if you have a temperature.
H It keeps you young.

Speaker 1 [6]
Speaker 2 [7]
Speaker 3 [8]
Speaker 4 [9]
Speaker 5 [10]

Unit 6

Use of English

Part 1 Multiple-choice cloze

1 Read the newspaper article below about a problem with the lack of sunlight in an Italian village. What solution helped to address this problem?

2 Read the article again and for questions 1–8, decide which answer (A, B, C or D) best fits each gap.

Brilliant idea lights up village

There is a village deep (0) ....**in**.... the foothills of the Italian Alps that until 2006 saw no sun for nearly three months every year. Since that year, however, its winters have been brightened by a giant mirror which reflects sunlight onto its (1) .... square.

Viganella is located in the (2) .... Antrona valley and the tailor-made sheet of steel had to be flown by helicopter to a (3) .... spot on the mountainside above the village. Mayor Pierfranco Midali, who led the project, first (4) .... the ball rolling with a comment made seven years earlier. He had told the architect who later designed the mirror that if he could (5) .... up with a solution to Viganella's problem, he would (6) .... it all the way.

Weighing more than a ton, and (7) .... on the nearby Colna Peak, the mirror lights up an area of 30 square metres for at least six hours a day. The manufacturer has (8) .... that it will withstand the strongest winds and last at least 30 years.

0	A at	B in	C under	D around
1	A first	B main	C important	D open
2	A narrow	B thin	C shallow	D slight
3	A concluded	B designated	C denoted	D specialised
4	A pushed	B had	C put	D set
5	A turn	B come	C make	D put
6	A hold	B bear	C support	D stand
7	A held	B positioned	C lain	D dropped
8	A guaranteed	B insured	C maintained	D assured

Unit 6 41

Review Units 4–6

1 Replace the words in italics with a suitable expression containing one of these words.

> hand   head   tongue   fingers   foot

a I *offended someone unintentionally* when I criticised the picture. I didn't realise Sue had painted it.
b I'm starving. Let's *go to* the nearest restaurant.
c Can anyone *help me* to carry these books to the library?
d There must be more to life than *working hard or for long hours* every day.
e What was that film we saw last week? *I can't remember at the moment.*

2 Correct the six mistakes with past tenses in this paragraph.

Example
University students ~~had~~ have made it their mission to save the Iberian lynx from extinction by undertaking a sponsored walk.

The students have become aware of the plight of the lynx when they had been starting some research into various species as part of their course. It has appeared that the lynx had being threatened by several factors. In recent years, their numbers were been depleted and their natural habitat has decreasing.

3 Choose the best word to complete a–f.

a Police have discovered that *counterfeit/copy* money was used to pay for the goods.
b Remember that whenever you need help, you can *count/calculate* on me.
c I have to confess that I deliberately *overheard/eavesdropped on* an extremely interesting conversation yesterday.
d The con man managed to *take/put* us in with his lies.
e What are you two *whispering/mumbling* about? What's the big secret?
f Kate could be an excellent student but spends too much time *sniggering/giggling* at silly jokes.

4 Complete sentences a–e using a suitable expression with *hold*.

a The film on TV last night was boring. It just didn't hold my .... at all.
b Hold the .... , will you? I'll see if Mr Jones is available.
c I shall hold you personally .... if anything goes wrong on the school trip.
d A woman has been held for .... in connection with the robbery.
e My parents are holding a .... for my 18th birthday.

5 Correct any incorrect negative prefixes in a–i.

a insteady   ....
b unviolent   ....
c unfortunate   ....
d inprecise   ....
e illegal   ....
f innatural   ....
g misorganised   ....
h non-understood   ....
i dispronounced   ....

6 Read the text below and correct the four mistakes with modals.

Jane Henley would not be happier after winning in the international track and field event at the age of 19. Her parents might have been delighted with her success. It mustn't have been easy making the sacrifices necessary for their daughter to realise her dream. They admitted they were very nervous, however, they needn't have worry!

42 Review Units 4–6

7 Complete the dialogues using *a*, *an*, *the* or no article.

1. A: Do you ever travel to work by .... train?
   B: Never – I prefer to go by .... bus or on .... foot.
2. A: What can .... governments do to help .... unemployed?
   B: They can increase .... unemployment benefits for .... start.
3. A: What do you think is .... main difference between .... British and .... French?
   B: Probably .... food they eat!
4. A: Were you at .... work when you heard .... news about the earthquake?
   B: I was at .... home watching TV.
5. A: I'll pick you up after .... dinner and we'll go to .... cinema.
   B: Fine – we'll have finished .... meal by about 7.30.
6. A: What does Jim want to do when he leaves .... school?
   B: He wants to join .... police force.
7. A: Do you have .... favourite flower?
   B: Yes – it's .... orchid.
8. A: What do you consider to be .... greatest invention ever?
   B: .... computer, of course.

8 Complete the adjectives below, then use these adjectives in sentences a–e.

- suspic............
- inform............
- court............
- malic............
- outrag............

a. David is extremely charming. I've never met anyone so .... and polite.
b. If you're confused about technology, read this book. It's .... and really useful.
c. The candidate failed to win due to the .... rumours the opposition had spread.
d. What's that man doing? He's behaving in a very .... manner.
e. She's one of the world's most .... singers and always causes controversy.

9 Rewrite this dialogue in indirect speech using the correct form of the reporting verbs in a–f. More than one answer may be possible.

Example
TED: What motivated you to become a safari guide?
Ted asked Sarah what had motivated her to become a safari guide. (ask)

SARAH: Ever since I was a child, I've been desperate to travel.
a .... (admit)

Have you ever been on safari?
b .... (ask)

TED: No, I haven't.
c .... (tell)

But it is one of my ambitions.
d .... (add)

SARAH: I hope one day you will go on one.
e .... (go on to say)

Why don't you take a place on my next trip?
f .... (offer)

10 Rewrite the second sentence in a–c keeping the meaning the same. Use between three to six words including the word given.

a. Bill said, 'I'll take you to the airport in my car'.
   GIVE
   Bill ....
   a lift to the airport.

b. Everyone believed my neighbour's claims about once being a famous singer.
   TAKEN
   Everyone ....
   my neighbour's claims about once being a famous singer.

c. What did you think about the exam? I couldn't understand the last question at all.
   HEAD
   What did you think about the exam? I couldn't
   ....
   the last question.

Review Units 4–6 43

Traces of the past

Reading

Part 6 Cross-text multiple matching

1 Quickly read the four extracts from reviews of the film *A field in England*. In which period of history is the film set?

2 Read the texts again. For questions 1–4, choose from the reviewers A–D. The reviewers may be chosen more than once.

Which reviewer, A, B, C or D:

takes a similar view to reviewer C regarding the circumstances of the film's release? 1 …

shares the same opinion as reviewer C about the film-maker's previous record? 2 …

expresses a different view from the others regarding the originality of the film? 3 …

has a different opinion from reviewer A regarding the old-fashioned presentation of the film? 4 …

A Nigel Andrews

This film's unprecedented multiple opening – simultaneously in theatres and on DVD and TV channel Film4 – suggests the film's creators think either 'Here is a commercial turkey, let's take the money and run' or 'Here is a new epoch of cinema. Everyone gather round.' I'll go with the second. This wonderful, bewildering movie from Ben Wheatley, scripted by wife-collaborator Amy Jump and set during the English Civil war, has put reviewers at sixes, sevens and any other number you can think of. Try to decode a plot in which a band of deserters, of both sides, stumble into a field being surveyed, mysteriously, by a treasure-seeking alchemist. The black-and-white photography, magically lit and textured, is like the primitive canvas on which the world starts to be daubed. The film begins in violence, ends in violence – a thieves-fall-out climax of multiple shootings – and in between traipses a landscape sown with the surreal, the symbolic, the fantastical.

B Geoffrey Macnab

Wheatley's macabre and funny previous film, *Sightseers*, was undermined by its cross-referencing of other movies and its casual sadism. Thankfully, here, he is not trying to hide behind British sardonic humour. There are rough patches. In its weaker moments, the film does resemble skits on movie genres. Nonetheless, once Michael Smiley's alchemist, O'Neil, hoves into view, the film-making takes on a new intensity. O'Neil is dressed exactly like Vincent Price's equally devilish character in Michael Reeves's *Witchfinder General* (1968). Influential horror historian David Pirie's description of Vincent Price as 'a superb presence of inexorable vindictiveness around which the other characters move with fascinated repulsion' could apply to Smiley's O'Neil. What is most refreshing about the film is its utterly offbeat quality. This is not another British project made to formulaic guidelines. Even the bloody final battle – which seems a bit like a spaghetti Western shootout transplanted to 17th-century rural England – confounds our expectations.

A field in England
Four reviewers comment on the film *A field in England*

C Roger Aldgate

Those expecting a quasi-documentary about the Civil War in England might be disappointed. Like *Sightseers*, a bizarre world of fact and fiction is what the film is about. Where the line between the two is drawn, however, is somewhat ambiguous. Ben Wheatley's film may seem at first sight to have been created out of a fervent desire to produce something out of the ordinary, but for all the attempts to present the film as a landmark cinema event, viewers may find the experience more bewildering than innovative. True, the promotion of the film is quite unlike any other, but the jury is still out regarding the verdict on the film itself. Wheatley has always tried, with varying degrees of success, to produce work which is both unnerving and controversial, but cinema-goers might find the monochrome setting less than gripping. How far the film succeeds in capturing the spirit of that period of history is debatable.

D Peter Bradshaw

A Field in England draws on a tradition that sees the English revolution as a period of visionary radicalism and insurrection, though here converted with cynicism and despair. All the digging and ranting is with something other than utopia in view. The monochrome images naturally call to mind a similar black-and-white picture, Kevin Brownlow's *Winstanley* (1976). The film's scriptwriter and co-editor is Amy Jump, Ben Wheatley's long-time collaborator; here they are working to create a more literary screenplay, without the improvised feeling of their earlier work. What a unique film-maker Wheatley is becoming. From the realms of contemporary realism, crime, comedy and fear, he has moved on to period drama, but cleverly alighted on the one period that suits his stripped-down visuals and subversive instincts perfectly.

Vocabulary

Phrasal verbs with *off* and *in*

1 Complete 1–5 with phrasal verbs formed from these verbs plus *off*.

■ take   bring   call   cut   show

1 During winter, the mountain villages are often .... by heavy snowstorms.
2 No-one expected Colin to organise the end-of-term party by himself, but he managed to .... it ....
3 Ted thinks he knows everything – he's always .... his expertise in something or other.
4 Plans for the wedding were unfortunately .... at the last minute as the bride fell in love with the best man.
5 Peterson's career really .... following the huge box-office hit of his first feature film.

2 Match the phrasal verbs from 1 with meanings a–e.

a end suddenly and unexpectedly
b succeed against expectations
c begin to be successful
d to be isolated
e try to impress people

3 Use the correct form of the verbs from 1 with the particle *in* to complete dialogues 1–5 below.

1 A: That's terrible – you must feel absolutely awful!
   B: I just can't believe it. I had to read his letter again and again to ....
2 A: Are you ready to talk to the candidates?
   B: Yes. Will you please .... them .... now?
3 A: Why were the police .... ?
   B: To investigate allegations of bribery and corruption.
4 A: More should be done to help one-parent families.
   B: But the government has only recently .... new measures to help them.
5 A: Have you met Andy's cousin? He's very rude.
   B: You can say that again. He always .... whenever someone tries to speak.

4 Match the phrasal verbs from 3 with meanings a–e.

a introduce
b bring here
c try to understand the meaning
d interrupt
e request to come and help

5 Choose the correct particle in sentences a–e to make a two-part phrasal verb.

a If you are told *in/off*, you have upset someone by doing something wrong or badly.
b If you take someone *in/off*, you let them stay at your house.
c If you go *in/off* something, you don't like it anymore.
d If you keep something *in/off*, you prevent yourself from saying what you think.
e If something pulls people *in/off*, it makes a lot of people want to see it.

Grammar
Reduced clauses

1 Complete the encyclopedia entry below using the correct participle form of the verbs in brackets.

The Atacama desert

1 .... (lie) between the high mountains of the Andes and the Pacific Ocean, and 2 .... (locate) in the northern part of Chile, the desert is the perfect terrain for preservation. 3 .... (bury) in the sand in prehistoric times, bodies can remain almost as intact as mummies.

4 .... (receive) less than 0.02 centimetres of rain a year – with some parts 5 .... (not/see) rainfall for the last 400 years – the Atacama desert is the most arid tract of land 6 .... (know). The area is favoured by scientists 7 .... (search) for the presence of water.

Grammar Extra
Suffixes

2 Match groups a–h with a suitable suffix. Remember you may have to change the spelling.

> -ess -hood -ship -ness
> -ist -less -ese -ful -ee

a train/employ/attend
b friend/relation/owner
c steward/act/host
d child/neighbour/likely
e happy/like/sweet
f special/capital/art
g care/hope/rest
h China/Portugal/Lebanon

3 Which group from 2 can take two suffixes?

4 Complete sentences a–l with the words in brackets and one of the suffixes below.

> -ian -cy -ment -ty

a (politics) Only one .... decided to back the revaluation of the currency yesterday.
b (content) They say that the secret of .... lies in leading a simple life.
c (anxious) The selection process caused great .... in applicants for the job.
d (music) Even a talented .... can have problems finding work.
e (clear) One of the most important qualities of effective writing is ....
f (fulfil) Vocational jobs such as teaching can bring great ....
g (democratic) .... means government by the people for the people.
h (argue) It is often difficult to make up after a heated ....
i (technical) Unfortunately the .... was unable to repair the computer.
j (secret) Each committee member must be sworn to .... prior to the ceremony.
k (authentic) Experts consider the .... of the manuscript to be under serious doubt.
l (diplomatic) Tact and .... are skills that are not easily learned.

Unit 7 47

Listening

Part 2 Sentence completion

1 Read the exam task in 2 and answer these questions.

a What was the item that was discovered?
b What was the name of the person who originally received it?

2 🎧 You will hear a talk about a discovery made by a librarian. For questions 1–8, complete the sentences.

A lucky find

Treasure hunting may be motivated by the media or a wish for (1) ....

The disadvantage of looking for valuable finds is that you may discover only a (2) ....

Some years ago a librarian discovered a manuscript that had been lying in an attic for (3) ....

The manuscript was written on (4) .... paper.

The librarian informed a well-known (5) .... and they arranged for an armoured car to collect the manuscript.

It was confirmed that the manuscript had been written in the author's (6) ....

The manuscript had originally been sent to the (7) .... of the librarian, Gluck.

Gluck's death meant that the manuscript was put away for another (8) .... to discover.

48 Unit 7

Use of English

Part 3 Word formation

1 Read the text below quickly to find out why this 'terracotta army' is so famous.

2 Read the text again and complete gaps 1–8 with the words given in capitals below.

The Terracotta Army

One of the most famous (0) *archaeological* finds must be the Terracotta Army. The clay figures that guard the tomb of the first Chinese (1) .... , Qin Shihuangdi, were actually found (2) .... by Chinese peasants digging a well.

Further (3) .... were carried out and it was shown that they had been placed around the tomb after Qin Shihuangdi's (4) ....

Qin Shihuangdi came to power at the age of thirteen and during his reign there were three attempts to (5) .... him. This may explain why, despite being so young, he had begun making (6) .... for an underground tomb to be built for after his death. Included were, of course, the (7) .... that made up the army.

The figures guarding the tomb were made with incredible attention to detail – each one has a face that is (8) .... and individual. For more than two thousand years, these figures have kept a continuous watch over the tomb.

0 ARCHAEOLOGY
1 EMPIRE
2 ACCIDENT
3 EXCAVATE
4 BURY
5 ASSASSIN
6 ARRANGE
7 WAR
8 MISTAKE

3 Write the correct forms of the words for a–j.

a the noun form of the adjective 'famous'
....
b the adjective form of the noun 'power'
....
c the verb form of the noun 'reign'
....
d the noun form of the verb 'explain'
....
e the noun form of past participle 'built'
....
f the adjective form of the noun 'detail'
....
g the adverb form of the noun 'figure'
....
h the adjective form of the verb 'watch'
....
i the noun form of 'credible'
....
j the noun form of the adjective 'continuous'
....

Unit 7

The big issues

8

Reading Part 5 Multiple choice

1 Read this extract from a book. How optimistic do you think the author is about the future of humankind?

2 For questions 1–6, read the extract again and choose the answer (A, B, C or D) which you think fits best according to the text.

1 The writer suggests in the first paragraph that agricultural development
 A may need to be carried out on other planets.
 B will one day be adequate to feed the world's population.
 C has had both positive and negative effects.
 D has played only a minor part in population growth.

2 When he states 'To put it another way' in line 11, the writer is
 A suggesting an alternative.
 B reinforcing an argument.
 C refuting an explanation.
 D expressing a different point of view.

3 In the second paragraph, the writer is casting doubt upon
 A the principal cause of climate change.
 B our understanding of the effect of burning fossil fuels.
 C the unpredictability of weather patterns.
 D our need for greener ways of regenerating energy.

4 What point does the writer make in the third paragraph?
 A The recent destruction of rainforests was no worse than any others.
 B More animals than plants are in danger of extinction in rainforests.
 C The true value of the rainforests is yet to be discovered.
 D The disappearance of forests is a relatively new phenomenon.

5 The writer uses the phrase 'woeful litany' in line 48 to illustrate
 A the distressing nature of the list of problems facing the world.
 B the length of the list of problems facing the world.
 C the effect various problems are having on the world.
 D the causes of the problems the world is facing.

6 In the last paragraph, the writer implies that
 A all generations have wanted a better future for their children.
 B the planet would never survive another population growth.
 C in the future we will find new freedoms to replace those we have lost.
 D under certain circumstances some continuation of our current lifestyle may be possible.

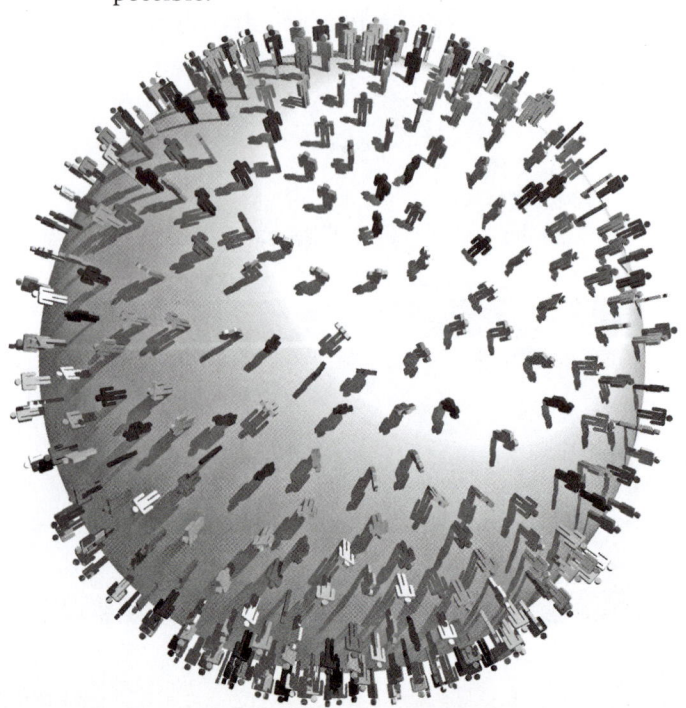

50 Unit 8

Our times

Since 1950, the global population has grown at up to a hundred times the speed it grew after the invention of agriculture, and ten thousand times as fast as it did before that. This is a great human achievement. The huge increase in population in the last century, and continuing in this, however, is a problem caused by success – the success of vaccination and clean-water programmes, and of the 'green revolution' in agriculture. Without the latter, it has been estimated that mankind would have needed extra farmland the size of North America to feed itself. To put it another way, some two billion people are alive because of it. Yet most observers believe so many billions of humans are too many for the planet to sustain indefinitely; we need too much water, we consume too much carbon-based energy, and we take over too much land to feed ourselves, for the biosphere to cope.

By far the best known problem in our world today is climate change. This is mainly caused by the burning of fossil fuels, which results in the production of greenhouse gas. This stops the planet cooling itself as efficiently as it needs to, thereby raising temperatures. By how much and exactly with what effect are unknown. An increase in 'wild' or unpredictable weather patterns may be one of the consequences. Looking at possible projections, this is either a problem rather over-stated today and which can be dealt with by greener ways of regenerating energy; or it is an imminent catastrophe that could make this the last human century.

Then there are the problems of deforestation and the extinction of species. Humans have always destroyed forests, both because they wanted the wood and to expand their farmland. Northern Europe was once covered in trees. But the deforestation of the 20th century was particularly dramatic, removing perhaps half of the remaining total; and was concentrated in tropical areas. The importance of forests for maintaining the health of the atmosphere, and coping with the carbon problem, is now well understood. In addition, these rainforests contain a high proportion of endangered plant and animal species, which may in turn harbour many useful secrets for human survival. If, as many scientists predict, around 30 per cent of current species become extinct over the next century, then that would be a huge planetary event, another mistake by the human ape.

Two last problems must be added to this woeful litany. Overfishing and the acidification of the oceans are causing an environmental disaster that would be a worldwide scandal if we were able to see clearly below the waves; and it is a disaster affecting an important source of food. Add to this the atmospheric pollution in the megacities that increasingly dominate as human habitations (more than half of us now live in cities), which has caused a huge loss of life, albeit generally in the older and weaker. The historian J. R. McNeill estimates a 20th century toll from air pollution of up to forty million people, equivalent to the combined casualties of both world wars, or about the same as the 1918–19 flu pandemic. Like other problems, this was a 'failure of success', in this case caused by the arrival of cars, air travel and a lifestyle more materially rich; many of those affected by pollution have migrated from villages and small towns and cities, prepared to live in slums or shanty towns simply to have the chance to exploit the greater opportunities of urban life.

Today's parents in the West are the first generation to worry that their children will live more meagre, if less wasteful, lives than they have. A world population of around today's size, or bigger, is plausible; and a wide range of scientific fixes, such as those mentioned for tackling global warming, and genetically modified food, would help the planet cope. What is not plausible is the notion of a bigger population enjoying the new freedoms of car use, air travel and foods flown in from around the globe that many of us now enjoy.

Vocabulary

Compound adjectives

1 Match groups a–f with 1–6 to make compound adjectives. Then use a dictionary to find four more compound adjectives beginning with *self*.

a half-/light-/broken-   1 minded
b open-/narrow-/broad-   2 made
c full-/part-/first-   3 handed
d left-/right-/single-   4 hearted
e over-/under-/un-   5 time
f man-/hand-/self-   6 stated

2 Use compound adjectives from 1 to complete sentences a–f. More than one answer may be possible.

a Due to current expansion, there are vacancies for two .... members of staff.
b These scissors are specially designed to be used by .... people.
c The new play at the Criterion theatre is a .... look at life in suburbia.
d He's so .... – he's not prepared to listen to anyone else's opinion.
e Have you seen these necklaces? They are all .... in Chile!
f The seriousness of the problem has been .... We have in fact come across very few problems.

Negative adjectives

3 Write the opposites of words a–h using a <u>negative</u> prefix.

a penetrable   *impenetrable*
b tolerable   ....
c perceptible   ....
d reversible   ....
e sensitive   ....
f stable   ....
g measurable   ....
h sociable   ....

4 Match the <u>opposites</u> from 3 with the similar meanings in 1–8 below. Check any words you are not sure of in a dictionary.

1 uncaring   5 indistinguishable
2 incalculable   6 unbearable
3 insecure   7 inaccessible
4 inhospitable   8 unchangeable

5 Complete sentences a–h with a suitable adjective from exercises 3 or 4. More than one answer may be possible.

a Which of these paintings is the original? They're completely .... to me.
b They're quite an .... family. They never really go out and mix with anyone.
c The heat is .... in here. I can't believe the air conditioning is still broken.
d Due to torrential weather conditions the mountain pass is .... via this route.
e My little sister is still quite .... and always seems to feel self-conscious.
f There are very few decisions in life that are .... in my experience.
g Torrel's work is known throughout the world – his contribution to the arts is ....
h I don't want to sound .... but it's time you sorted out your own mistakes!

Unit 8

Grammar

Conditionals

1 Look at the picture of the man and complete sentences a–e with a suitable conditional phrase using the verb in brackets.

Example

<u>He would not have slipped</u> (slip) if he hadn't gone so close to the edge.

a If he shouts for help, no one .... (hear) him.

b If he .... (take) a photo, he wouldn't be in trouble!

c If he could reach his mobile, he .... (call) for help.

d If he .... (reach) the tree, he could climb to safety.

e If he had told someone where he was, they .... (find) him.

2 Rewrite these conditional sentences using the prompts given.

a My aunt lent me the money, so I was able to go abroad.
If my aunt ....

b Never stay out in the midday sun because of the risk of getting burned.
If you ....

c Thomas had three jobs over the summer and then he was able to buy a motorbike.
If Thomas ....

d It's not certain that I can offer you a scholarship, but I'd like to know how you feel about it.
If I were ....

e Profits are down because demand for our products is falling.
If demand ....

3 Complete these conditional sentences using the correct form of the verb in brackets.

a When petrol .... (ignite), it .... (go up) in flames.

b If I .... (know) the answer to your question, I .... (tell) you.

c I .... (gain) lots of experience if I .... (volunteer) for the project – but I didn't apply.

d If visibility .... (not/be) poor last night, the flight .... (leave) on time.

e .... (let) me know if you .... (like) me to cook dinner tonight.

f If Jack .... (not/work) so hard at university, he .... (not/get) such a good degree.

g If only you .... (not/argue) with your boss! If you .... (keep) quiet, you .... (not/got) the sack!

Unit 8   53

Listening Part 3 Multiple choice

1 What do you already know about 'artificial intelligence'? Do you think these developments in technology are important for our lives?

2 🎧 You will hear a radio interview with Paul Williams, an expert in artificial intelligence. For questions 1–6, choose the answer which fits best according to what you hear.

1 Paul explains that predictions made about AI in the past
  A turned out to be surprisingly accurate.
  B proved to be a long way off-target.
  C overestimated the demand for computers.
  D underestimated the 'brain power' of computers.

2 According to Paul, how do most experts feel about the future of AI?
  A convinced it could soon govern every aspect of our lives
  B uncertain what impact it might eventually have on our lives
  C worried that its development may get out of control
  D certain that its full effects will not be seen for some time yet

3 Paul feels that the comparison of AI and the arrival of the computer industry
  A shows that both industries are at a similar state of development.
  B illustrates that the computer industry was more popular in its time than AI.
  C misrepresents the true role of AI in our lives.
  D proves that the computer industry was a much more profitable concern.

4 What does Paul believe people's attitudes were to new technology in the 1900s?
  A They were very excited about its potential.
  B They had little idea what impact it would have.
  C They were suspicious of how it might change their lives.
  D They expected it to develop more quickly than it did.

5 Paul is slightly worried by the fact that machines which have intelligence could
  A one day kill off human beings.
  B rapidly assume human roles.
  C eventually replace humans in the workplace.
  D be running our lives in the near future.

6 What conclusion does Paul finally reach?
  A Science fiction is closer to reality than we think.
  B Intelligent machines will be able to feel emotions.
  C AI will develop more rapidly than we can ever imagine.
  D We should not be afraid that technology will take over our lives.

Unit 8

Use of English Part 1 Multiple-choice cloze

1 Read the article below, ignoring the gaps, about a survey into volunteering. Why do people and businesses want to become involved?

2 For questions 1–8, read the article again and decide which answer (A, B, C or D) best fits each gap.

WHAT'S IN IT FOR ME?

Students and jobseekers keen to get onto the course or into the workplace of their (0) ...B... hope that voluntary work will help them (1) .... out from the crowd. This chance to gain experience is (2) .... on the wish-list of young people.

Surveys reveal that young and old (3) .... find that volunteering improves their lives, particularly when they are involved in conservation or heritage work.

Businesses often encourage volunteering; staff get a break from their daily routine and also develop 'soft skills' such as initiative and decision-making. One volunteering organisation is (4) .... a survey to find out if volunteering does make a difference in the workplace, or if it is something businesses do simply to improve their (5) ....

Not (6) .... are business-sponsored placements becoming more common, the government is also investing in a scheme to (7) .... volunteers. The more people who participate, the more the act fulfils its (8) .... of making the world a better place.

0	A alternative	B choice	C option	D election
1	A stand	B lift	C pick	D point
2	A extreme	B high	C sharp	D strong
3	A similar	B the same	C alike	D too
4	A governing	B guiding	C conducting	D directing
5	A representation	B look	C image	D figure
6	A only	B just	C merely	D simply
7	A reinforce	B recruit	C restore	D renew
8	A aim	B direction	C mark	D design

3 Decide which answer (A, B, C or D) best fits each gap in 1–6.

1 My husband .... the 'Employee of the Year' award!
  A won B achieved C acquired D gained

2 The government .... out a survey last year into the benefits of volunteering.
  A worked B found C carried D turned

3 The company has been .... in this kind of scheme for over a year now.
  A committed B associated C connected D involved

4 The management needs to .... out the real cause of discontent among the staff.
  A carry B find C make D turn

5 The new contract has .... strong emotions within the workforce.
  A raised B increased C aroused D motivated

6 Our productivity is low .... staff motivation is low.
  A although B because C whereas D while

9 It's a crime

Reading

Part 8 Multiple matching

1 Quickly read the text, which reviews several books, and find out in which country each novel is set.

2 Read the text again and decide in which book review (A–F) the following are mentioned. The reviews may be chosen more than once.

a plot that is rather unusual for the writer in question	1 …
the best novel the writer has produced so far	2 …
a desire to make international literature more accessible	3 …
a novel that it is impossible to stop reading	4 …
a past era accurately captured by the writer	5 …
a crime against a family of considerable importance	6 …
a storyline that deliberately misleads the reader	7 …
a family who have come down in the world	8 …
a character wanting a say in running the country	9 …
a character who reacts against their social background	10 …

FAMILIES

A

A remarkable young woman makes the first of what I hope will be many appearances in Denise Mina's *The Field of Blood*. It's 1981 and Paddy Meehan, eighteen, is determined that her lowly job as a copygirl on a Scottish
5 newspaper will be her first step to becoming a reporter. It's an aspiration that separates her from her working-class Catholic parents, who are suspicious of ambition and want everything to continue as it always has. When two small boys are arrested for the murder of a toddler, Paddy
10 believes that the police don't have the whole story, and conducts her own investigation. But this is not simply a murder mystery. Mina produces something special every time and this book – her finest yet – offers a memorable portrait of a touching heroine, along with the dynamics of
15 the workplace and, especially, the family.

56 Unit 9

B

Barbara Vine also uses crime as one element in her books. She is in unusually gentle mood in *The Minotaur*, in which a Swedish woman describes an unsettling experience that happened over 30 years before, when she was engaged to look after the grown-up son of a bizarre English household. The once grand, now shabby house, is ruled by a tyrannical old woman, whose three unmarried daughters lead separate, dismal lives, moving cautiously around their autistic brother. The narrative is as compelling, but not as dark, as we have come to expect from this distinguished author.

C

The latest addition to Bitter Lemon Press is prize-winning Cuban novelist Leonardo Padura. He does nothing to hinder their mission to publish English translations of the best foreign crime fiction. *Havana Red*, the first book in his Havana quartet, introduces Lieutenant Mario Conde – an eccentric personality with unusual investigative methods. All his skills are called upon when a murder victim turns out to be the son of a prominent diplomat. Padura's powerful writing creates an atmospheric picture of a turbulent city, illuminated by Conde's mocking commentary.

AND OTHER CRIMINALS

D

Jess Walter continues to impress with his new novel *Citizen Vince*, which takes place in the run-up to the 1980 US Presidential election. His protagonist, Vince Camden, is a life-long criminal who has avoided another prison sentence by giving evidence against other criminals. He is in witness protection, contentedly managing a doughnut shop, while keeping his hand in with a little credit card fraud, when he discovers that his life is in danger. Vince suddenly realises not only that he enjoys his new life but that, for the first time, it is important to him to vote in an election. His attempts to dodge his assassin and pay off his debts so that he can cast his vote make a splendidly entertaining, thoughtful book.

E

John Lawton's post-Second World War series features the London-based policeman Frederick Troy. Troy is upper-class and his friends and colleagues include both influential figures of society, and faithful (though sometimes less than law-abiding) members of the lower classes. Lawton's plots are tough and Troy spends much of his time in bed, in hospital or getting to know various female characters. In *Blue Rondo*, we have reached the 1950s and Troy, now a Chief Superintendent, is investigating a gangland war whilst recovering from yet another injury and … other subplots! Lawton's period atmosphere, illustrated with credible characters, is impeccable and the writing elegantly precise.

F

Harlan Coben has made his intentions clear: he wants to give his protagonist – the good guy – a hard time. And he makes a good job of doing so in *The Innocent*. Everything is going well for Matt Hunter; he has a great job, his wife is expecting their first baby, and they have their ideal American home. But then he finds his life and marriage inexplicably threatened by an unknown man. The enjoyably intricate plot takes several turns, involving a videotape, FBI agents, and even a dead nun, before we are taken on a final twist when the villains and motive are revealed. A book you can't help reading in one go.

Vocabulary

Phrasal verbs: multiple particles

1 Read the different definitions for phrasal verbs with *fall*. Then use a dictionary to find the correct particle for each definition a–g.

fall		
	a	be tricked into believing something that is not true
	b	have something to use when you are in difficulty
	c	try very hard or want very much to do something
	d	to not be completed or not happen
	e	fail to keep up with something
	f	decrease in quality or quantity
	g	have an argument with someone so that you are no longer friendly with them

2 Complete dialogues 1–7 using the phrasal verbs from 1.

1. A: I'm afraid I've .... with my work this week.
   B: Oh, you'll easily catch up over the weekend.

2. A: Did you manage to find anyone interested in joining the student committee?
   B: Not really – people weren't exactly .... We have to make it sound more appealing.

3. A: What on earth will I do if the new business doesn't take off?
   B: You can always .... your teaching qualifications – don't worry!

4. A: Did you get that job you wanted with the travel agency?
   B: I didn't. At the last minute the whole thing .... because they filled the vacancy with an internal candidate.

5. A: Do you get on well with the neighbours?
   B: No. We .... over a year ago and we haven't spoken since.

6. A: I can't believe that you .... that story about Jack being a pilot.
   B: Neither can I – but it seemed plausible at the time.

7. A: Why isn't the football team getting any funding now?
   B: Well, hardly anyone is going to the matches. Attendance has really .... over the last few months.

Unit 9

Grammar

Passives

1 Read the text about an arts academy. Then rewrite each sentence beginning with the words in bold and using the passive form.

BOWLANDS ACADEMY OF ARTS

Someone established **Bowlands Academy of Arts** five years ago. The Department of Education has now officially recognised **the establishment**. The academy offers students **a programme of short, intensive courses**, as well as three-year degree courses. Students can take **a range of examinations** throughout the year. Staff instruct **students** in small groups and they assign every student a personal tutor. Anyone requiring **accommodation in a hall of residence** must book it in advance. Students need to enclose **a deposit** with the enrolment form. The Academy will request **the balance** before the course starts. Students need to inform **the Academy** immediately if they intend to withdraw from their course.

Example
Bowlands Academy of Arts was established five years ago.

2 Complete dialogues 1–7 using the prompts in brackets and a verb below in the correct form.

> steal   service   investigate   confiscate
> pierce   dry-clean   test

1 A: I can't read the small print in this document.
　B: Maybe you should go to the optician's and .... (get/eyes) ....
2 A: What's Jill done to herself? She looks different.
　B: It's the earrings. She .... (have/ears) .... last week.
3 A: Look at this stain on my sleeve!
　B: You'll have to .... (get/jacket) ....
4 A: I'd forgotten I had this pair of scissors in my hand-luggage.
　B: They're bound to .... (get) .... by airport security staff.
5 A: The engine won't start.
　B: I don't believe it. We only .... (have/car) .... last week.
6 A: The central locking's broken so I've had to leave the car unlocked.
　B: Let's hope it .... (not/get) ....
7 A: Have you heard anything more about that enormous tax bill you were sent?
　B: Actually, I .... (have/matter) .... by my accountant at this very moment.

3 Rewrite statements a–e using the passive form of the word in italics and beginning with the prompts given.

a There's a *rumour* that the government is going to resign.
　It ....
b Financial experts *predict* interest rates are about to rise.
　Interest rates ....
c Everyone *assumed* the missing gangland leader had been murdered.
　The missing ....
d They *think* the plane crash was due to human error.
　It ....
e People *believe* terrorists are hiding out in the north of the country.
　Terrorists ....

Unit 9

Listening Part 1 Multiple choice

1 Discuss these questions which relate to the extracts in exercise 2.

   a   What types of discipline are typically used in schools in your country?
   b   Is antisocial behaviour a problem in schools or in public places where you live? How do you think this should be dealt with?

2 🎧 Read questions 1–6 below before you listen to the three different extracts. Then listen and choose the answer (A, B or C) which fits best according to what you hear.

extract one
You hear part of an interview with a teacher talking about 'the cooler room'.

1 'The cooler room' has attracted a lot of publicity because it
   A is seen as a controversial punishment.
   B has a link with a famous film.
   C shows an old-fashioned approach to discipline.

2 The punishment has been effective because pupils
   A dislike being constantly watched.
   B do not like being on their own.
   C hate the restrictions imposed on them.

extract two
You hear two people on a current affairs programme talking about ASBOs (Antisocial Behaviour Orders).

3 What do ASBOs do?
   A give a short prison sentence
   B offer help to offenders
   C restrict people's movements

4 The problem with ASBOs is that they
   A are not always obeyed.
   B can be given to the wrong people.
   C do not last long enough.

extract three
You hear part of an interview with a woman from the Witness Support Programme.

5 Why can giving evidence be distressing?
   A It's frightening to face criminals.
   B It's something you can't prepare for.
   C It can bring back bad memories.

6 The majority of people who work on the Programme
   A work unusual hours.
   B do not receive payment.
   C have special training.

Unit 9

Use of English Part 2 Open cloze

1 Read the description below of the film *Ocean's Twelve* and find out what type of film it is.

2 For questions 1–8, read the text again and think of the word which best fits each gap.

Ocean's Twelve

The film *Ocean's Eleven* (and (0) ...by... that, I mean the remake) had an indefinable quality. Now we have a sequel which feels too much (1) .... a clone of the first one.

Three years after the first daring robbery, Danny Ocean is living out a quiet retirement. But one day, (2) .... should arrive at his front door but Terry Benedict, the man (3) .... whom Ocean's Eleven stole a fortune. (4) .... though the insurance company paid him in full for his loss, he wants the money back – with the interest. Terry has managed to hunt down the rest of Ocean's gang and he wants nearly two million dollars within two weeks, (5) .... they will die.

There's (6) .... choice, really, so the crew heads for Amsterdam. There they have a contact who offers them a chance to make the money they need. It is at this point that *Ocean's Twelve*, however, comes (7) .... as being far too complicated. Perhaps it tries too hard, maybe it's not trying hard (8) ...., or possibly both.

Part 4 Key word transformations

3 For a–d, complete the second sentence so that it has a similar meaning to the first sentence, using the word given. Use between three and six words.

a I don't think you'll find a better deal for car insurance.
  CHANCES
  The .... find a better deal for car insurance.

b Our latest project presented us with many problems.
  AGAINST
  During our latest project we .... many problems.

c The issue will be investigated next week without fail.
  LOOKED
  The issue is .... next week without fail.

d I'm still waiting for you to repay the money I lent you six months ago.
  BACK
  You still .... the money I lent you six months ago.

Unit 9 61

Review Units 7–9

1 Match 1–7 with a–f to make compound adjectives.

1 narrow-   a handed
2 self-   b time
3 down   c hearted
4 first-   d minded
5 open-   e made
6 over   f stated
7 light-

2 Complete the text about astronomy by putting the words in brackets into a suitable participle form.

(1 peer) .... for years across 1,500 light years of space, scientists now believe they may have found an explanation for creation.
(2 use) .... a sophisticated telescope, scientists have studied hundreds of stars,
(3 identify) .... 27 that behave as the sun did 4.6 billion years ago. The nine planets around the sun were the only ones (4 know) .... in the whole universe, but (5 make) .... use of recent observations, astronomers then began to detect other planets. (6 conclude) .... their research, scientists believe they may have discovered the beginnings of earth-like planets.

3 Complete these sentences using the correct form of *fall* with a suitable particle.

a What's it like to be head-over-heels in love? I've never .... anybody.
b Never .... with your studies. If you do, you'll never catch up.
c When the sale started, crowds of customers were .... to grab a bargain.
d The skiing trip .... in the end, as it proved too complicated to arrange.
e Things haven't been so pleasant here since we .... with the neighbours in the flat above.
f Surely you didn't .... that ridiculous story? It was obvious he was lying!

4 Complete sentences a–f with words formed by adding suffixes to 1–6.

1 neighbour
2 care
3 act
4 employ
5 friend
6 child

a Sally won .... of the month at her office!
b I think socialising and forming new .... are the most enjoyable parts of my life.
c I spent my .... in Scotland; it was an amazing place to grow up.
d Nicole Kidman is my favourite .... I adore all her films.
e This .... is very exclusive; it's an extremely affluent area.
f He is unbelievably .... with his work and continuously makes mistakes.

5 Complete a–g with an appropriate phrasal verb in the correct form.

a Why aren't you and Andrew speaking? Have you .... with each other?
b Please don't put any onions in the casserole. I used to like them but I'm afraid I .... them recently.
c If you .... with your schedule, you'll find it very difficult to keep up with your work.
d The children got .... by our neighbour for breaking his window with their football.
e Maybe we'll have to .... lodgers to make a little more cash.
f A good education is something that you can always .... in times of trouble.
g No one expected the film to do well but it really .... in a big way.

6 Write the correct phrasal verb with *off* or *in* for definitions a–g.

a understand or remember sth t..............
b try to impress people s..............
c ask for sb's services c..............
d suddenly become successful t..............
e introduce a new law b..............
f interrupt sb when speaking c..............
g succeed in doing sth difficult b..............

7 Add the correct negative prefix to adjectives 1–8, then match them with synonyms a–h.

1 ....tolerable   a inaccessible
2 ....reversible   b inhospitable
3 ....stable   c indistinguishable
4 ....sensitive   d insecure
5 ....sociable   e incalculable
6 ....penetrable   f unbearable
7 ....perceptible   g uncaring
8 ....measurable   h unchangeable

8 Underline the correct conditional form in sentences a–h.

a If I *would have/had* enough free time, I would do voluntary work.
b If she *asks/had asked* me, I'll consider helping out at the festival.
c If they *had left/leave* home earlier, they would not have missed the train.
d If students *read/would read* English newspapers, it helps improve their vocabulary.
e If you *see/had seen* Ben this morning, remind him to pick up those tickets.
f If I *went/had visited* Australia, I might have emigrated permanently.
g If the restaurant *was/wasn't* so expensive, we could go there for our anniversary.
h If only I *didn't buy/hadn't bought* that second-hand car – it's been nothing but trouble.

9 Complete the gaps a–g in the table with the correct form of the words given.

Noun	Adjective
a	content
b anxiety	....
c clarity	....
d	secret
e diplomacy	....
f	authentic
g democracy	....

10 Correct the mistakes in the passive form in a–g.

a The package was arrived safely and on schedule this morning.
b Tonight's recital is been given by a well-known pianist.
c Exhibit 451 is being thought to have been painted by Picasso.
d This violin is to be considered the best example of a period instrument of this kind.
e I can't stand having made to do what I consider to be a waste of time.
f A collection of priceless gold coins has being discovered in a castle on the south coast.
g According to the police, this building could have abandoned for some time.

11 Rewrite the second sentence in a–c keeping the meaning the same. Use three to six words including the word given.

a Remote parts of the country always become isolated in severe weather.
CUT
Remote parts of the country ....
.... in severe weather.

b Apparently the entire warehouse was destroyed in a fire last month.
UP
Apparently the entire warehouse ....
.... last month.

c You should go for an eye test if you're struggling to read the newspaper.
TESTED
You should ....
if you're struggling to read the newspaper.

Review Units 7–9

Buying and selling

Reading Part 7 Gapped text

1 Quickly read the article about the textile industry in China. What facts or figures do you find surprising?

2 Read the article again. Six paragraphs have been removed from the extract. Choose from the paragraphs A–G the one which fits each gap (1–6). There is one extra paragraph which you do not need to use.

dressing for success

The next time you get dressed, think about Qiaotou. Whether you are wearing jeans or a skirt, the chances are that the button or zip comes from this unassuming, dusty town. It is too small to be on most western maps, too insignificant to appear in newspapers, and is barely known outside the local area. But in just a couple of decades this humble Chinese community has become the global capital of buttons and zips.

1 ....

The commercial revolution here is on an unprecedented scale. The first workshop was established in 1980 by three brothers who picked their first buttons off the street. Now the town's 700 family-run factories produce 15 billion buttons and 200 million metres of zips annually. The low-investment, labour-intensive industry was ideal for this remote community. And the timing was perfect. Qiaotou began popping buttons just as China started dressing up. Out went the Mao suits, and in came chic western clothes. So if you want any kind of button to adorn your new fashions, this is the place to come.

2 ....

Such mind-boggling export statistics, at least initially, were seen as evidence of the Chinese miracle. After the Cultural Revolution, the world cheered on the market-oriented reforms. Growth of around 9% a year for over two decades lifted many millions out of poverty. And consumers across the globe have benefited from cheap goods made by workers in Qiaotou and elsewhere.

3 ....

But Chinese businessmen are unfazed by this action. 'Even if we lose a few customers in the short term, they will have to come back,' says the president of the Great Wall Zipper group. 'There is almost nowhere else in the world that makes zips.'

4 ....

Take, for instance, Yiwu. If China is the workshop of the world, Yiwu is its showroom. Selling everything from engine parts to jewellery, this town's market has grown from a few street stalls to become the world's biggest commodity trading centre.

5 ....

It is hard to imagine this worldwide monopoly will end soon; Lanswe, the biggest global sock manufacturer, produces two million socks a day. Within two years the company plans to triple its workforce and increase output to five million socks a day, half of which are destined for export.

6 ....

The view from China is that foreign countries say they want China to develop, but when it does, they become nervous. China is changing and change is a cause for hope. But China needs to be given time to make sure its miracle does not sour.

Unit 10

A

And international buyers do indeed come here. Attracted by low prices and decent quality, retail outlets and fashion houses are increasingly purchasing from Qiaotou. The local chamber of commerce estimates that three out of every five buttons in the world are made in the town, which ships around two million zips a day, the highest quota of China's 80% share of the world-wide zip market.

B

Talk of unfair currency manipulation is nothing new. The domination of the world markets for cars and electronics in the 1980s led to a fierce trade dispute and pressure for appreciation of the yen. When this happened, the flood of money into the country inflated a speculative bubble in the early 90s.

C

Thus a modest village became a manufacturing powerhouse – a microcosm of what has happened to the Chinese economy in the last few decades. Paddy fields were cleared for factories and peasants have become industrialists. The river, once a clean source for irrigation, is now a heavily polluted outlet for plastic waste.

D

The same confidence prevails throughout the southern provinces. With endless streets of giant factories and company dormitories, the most developed areas are reminiscent of Western cities during the Industrial Revolution. The small towns have become world-beaters by focusing on labour-intensive niches.

E

The company's president understands why countries might restrict this growth and impose limits, even though it damages his business. 'But, even if the yuan gets stronger, rich countries will import socks because they cannot make them cheaply themselves.' He believes change must come through market forces rather than export quotas and currency manipulation. 'To compete with China, the wealthier nations need to make us richer. That's the way to make prices rise here.'

F

Towns like this one grew almost unnoticed, but the world now sees how powerful they have become. Thanks to globalisation, the world's clothes are zipped and buttoned up by migrant workers, our teeth are brushed with bristles from Huang Zi, and our toes are warmed by the products of Yiwu.

G

But recently, warnings have replaced the rejoicing. Chinese goods have flooded international markets, threatening jobs and alarming governments. One administration responded by setting a limit on shipments of certain items. Others have acted less aggressively, setting quotas to protect their clothing industries from Chinese competition.

Vocabulary

Money

1 The three words given in each of 1–4 have a similar meaning. Complete sentences a and b with the most suitable word from the three given.

1 fees/invoices/fares
   a Taxi .... usually increase dramatically after midnight.
   b Entrance .... to the gallery are reduced for students.
2 bill/receipt/cheque
   a You will need to obtain a .... to claim your expenses.
   b I didn't expect to receive such a large .... !
3 pay/salary/wage
   a The introduction of the minimum .... was welcomed by all employees.
   b His annual .... fell just below the national average.
4 cash/change/tip
   a We need to resolve the business's .... flow problems within the next month.
   b Do you have any loose .... to pay for the coffees?

2 Complete sentences a–d with words from 1 in the correct form.

a .... for manual work are still way behind those of skilled workers.
b Tuition .... are one of many issues facing students today.
c Have you got some .... to leave a tip for the waiter?
d Make sure that you get a .... when you pay for the goods.

Word formation

3 Write the verb forms of a–i, ending in *-ate*, *-en*, or *-ify*. Use a dictionary to help you.

a false ....
b strength ....
c activity ....
d broad ....
e typical ....
f alternative ....
g demonstration ....
h sad ....
i peace ....

4 Use the verbs from 3 in the correct form to complete these sentences.

a Opposition to our plans .... and increased our determination to put them into action.
b To be fluent in another language, you should .... the vocabulary you learn by using it as often as possible.
c It later became apparent that the documentation had been .... and we had all been misled.
d The mood of the waiting crowd .... between boredom and anger.
e Can you find a way to .... the region and resolve the conflict?
f We were all .... to hear about the loss of your grandfather, and send our sympathy.
g After working in the same city for ten years, I decided to .... my horizons and travel the world.

Grammar Mixed conditionals

1 Make conditional sentences from the boxes below. There may be more than one possibility.

a Permission for the event will not be given		it's an emergency.
b What you may have done in the past is not important	unless	you are honest with me now.
	provided	I wanted you to be involved in it?
c I never use my mobile phone	as long as	he'd been forced to.
d Would you agree to the scheme	supposing	all safety regulations are complied with.
e Jim would never have changed his job		

2 Choose the correct option, a or b, to complete sentences 1–7.

1 Don't you wish you .... speak more languages fluently?
   a could   b would

2 I wish I .... afford to upgrade my computer system.
   a would be able to   b could

3 My brother wishes he .... the firm he is currently working for.
   a didn't join   b hadn't joined

4 If only my boss .... me to work all day long.
   a haven't expected   b didn't expect

5 Do you ever wish you .... to go somewhere else on holiday?
   a had chosen   b chose

6 If only people .... keep interrupting me in mid-sentence!
   a won't   b wouldn't

7 I wish I .... to your advice.
   a wouldn't listen   b hadn't listened

Grammar Extra Determiners

3 Circle the correct determiner to complete sentences a–j.

a *The whole/All the* idea of raising money to keep run-down museums open seems pointless.
b There is *not many/hardly any* good news in the media these days.
c The question of whether we can actually help developing countries by giving aid is a difficult *one/other*.
d *None/Neither* of the advice that Charlotte offered was useful to me.
e *Every/Each* of the paintings on loan for the exhibition has been insured against damage.
f Unfortunately, due to my family commitments, I have *a little/little* time to myself these days.
g *Loads/Several* of people came to the opening of the Italian restaurant.
h Some traffic restrictions do prevent accidents, whereas *others/another* merely cause traffic jams.
i Fortunately, *a few/few* people managed to make it to work yesterday, despite the atrocious weather conditions.
j The *most/whole* we can do is hope they don't notice our mistakes.

Unit 10 67

Listening Part 3 Multiple choice

1 What problems or consequences do you think 'music piracy' (illegally obtaining music) may cause?

2 🎧 You will hear an interview with a journalist, Sam Broadbent, who is talking about music piracy. For questions 1–6, choose the correct answers.

1 According to Sam, the issue of music piracy is complicated because
   A too many private individuals are being taken to court.
   B it's unclear who should actually be prosecuted.
   C it's difficult to prevent people buying the necessary software.
   D the entertainment industry is making downloading too desirable.

2 What happened in one legal case in 1984?
   A The use of video recorders was banned in certain places.
   B The entertainment industry successfully sued a video manufacturer.
   C It was decided that the main purpose of video recording was not illegal.
   D A video manufacturer was found guilty of making illegal copies of films.

3 Sam says the current legal case
   A concentrates on the many people losing their income.
   B doesn't question how the products are used.
   C is targeting the firms that enable people to download illegally.
   D suggests the banning of illegal products.

4 What is Sam's greatest fear?
   A People will stop worrying about whether downloading is right or wrong.
   B The development of downloading technology will be slowed.
   C People in the entertainment industry will no longer be active.
   D Manufacturers of new technology will constantly be involved in lawsuits.

5 According to Sam, many members of the public he has talked to feel that
   A copyright laws should be further tightened.
   B the products they buy could be less expensive.
   C the entertainment industry is losing out financially.
   D distribution costs should be passed on to the manufacturers.

6 In Sam's opinion, films should be released
   A much more quickly on DVD.
   B in Europe before being released in the USA.
   C on the Internet and at the cinema at the same time.
   D in cinemas all over the world simultaneously.

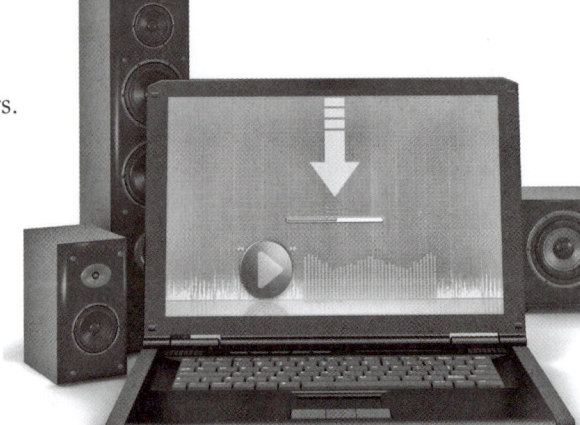

Use of English

Part 3 Word formation

1 Read the article below about 'Freecycle' and find out what it is and how it started.

2 For questions 1–8, read the text again and use the words given in capitals to form a word that fits in the gap.

Giving it away

Craving a new outfit or a little treat is an understandable (0) ......*indulgence*...... and resisting the (1) .... urge to buy one is hard. Nowadays, however, guilty shoppers can get rid of (2) .... purchases by simply giving them away online using organisations such as Freecycle. These organisations help to reduce the amount of rubbish sent to landfill sites through the (3) .... of a more efficient form of recycling. Whether it's a CD, old jeans or a broken bicycle, the free item will be (4) .... to someone!

Freecycle is the creation of Deron Beal, an (5) .... from Arizona. Today, it is a cross between an internet auction house and a (6) .... chain of charity shops. Beal says his aim is to cut waste. 'I live in a beautiful desert area,' he explained to (7) .... , 'and in the middle is this hideous landfill, overflowing with good, reusable stuff.' The Freecycle Network now has millions of members worldwide. So, if you want a sofa in (8) .... good condition, and the owner lives nearby, it can be picked up rather than posted!

0 INDULGE
1 IMPULSE
2 WANT
3 PROMOTE
4 VALUE
5 ENVIRONMENT
6 GLOBE
7 REPORT
8 REASON

3 For a–e, complete the sentences with the correct forms of the word given.

a RESIST

I love buying second-hand goods. I find them ....

The polar bear shows impressive .... to extremely cold temperatures.

b EFFICIENT

The recycling process in this town is very .... Surely it can be improved.

I was impressed by the speed and .... of the new machinery.

c FREE

What I value more than anything is my ....

I hope you feel that you can speak .... to me about the issue.

d USE

Many of these items are .... , so don't throw them away!

This gadget is terrible – it's the most .... thing I've ever had in the kitchen!

e EXPLAIN

Various people have given .... of the process, but I still don't understand it.

If the reasons for my resignation are not clear, I would be happy to write an .... letter.

Unit 10 69

11 Entertainment or art?

Reading

Part 6 Cross-text multiple matching

1 Quickly read the texts opposite. What are the writers talking about?

2 Read the texts again. For questions 1–4, choose from the writers A–D. The writers may be chosen more than once.

Which writer, A, B, C or D:

takes a similar view to writer A regarding the frequency of taking photographic images? 1 …

has a different opinion from writer C about modern methods of taking photographs? 2 …

expresses a different view from the others regarding the impact of old family photos? 3 …

shares writer A's feelings regarding the storage of photographic images? 4 …

Snap Happy

A Grayson Perry, artist

After compact automatic cameras became available I took a lot of snaps, particularly when my daughter was young. This was a habit I kept up until fairly recently. I used to put them
5 lovingly in albums, until I saw a TV programme which pointed out that those clingfilm-style albums are terrible for the prints. I found this very disconcerting, so I now keep them in a shoebox. Since the advent of digital
10 photography, I have taken fewer and fewer photos for fun, but hugely more for research, or to record my work. I take a few when I go on holiday but return with just a dozen snaps. I don't know whether this is because of
15 age, laziness or the feeling that photography has become a torrent of clichés. The camera-phone has made the forest of glowing screens ubiquitous at events. Maybe I'm a snob, but it's put me off photography.

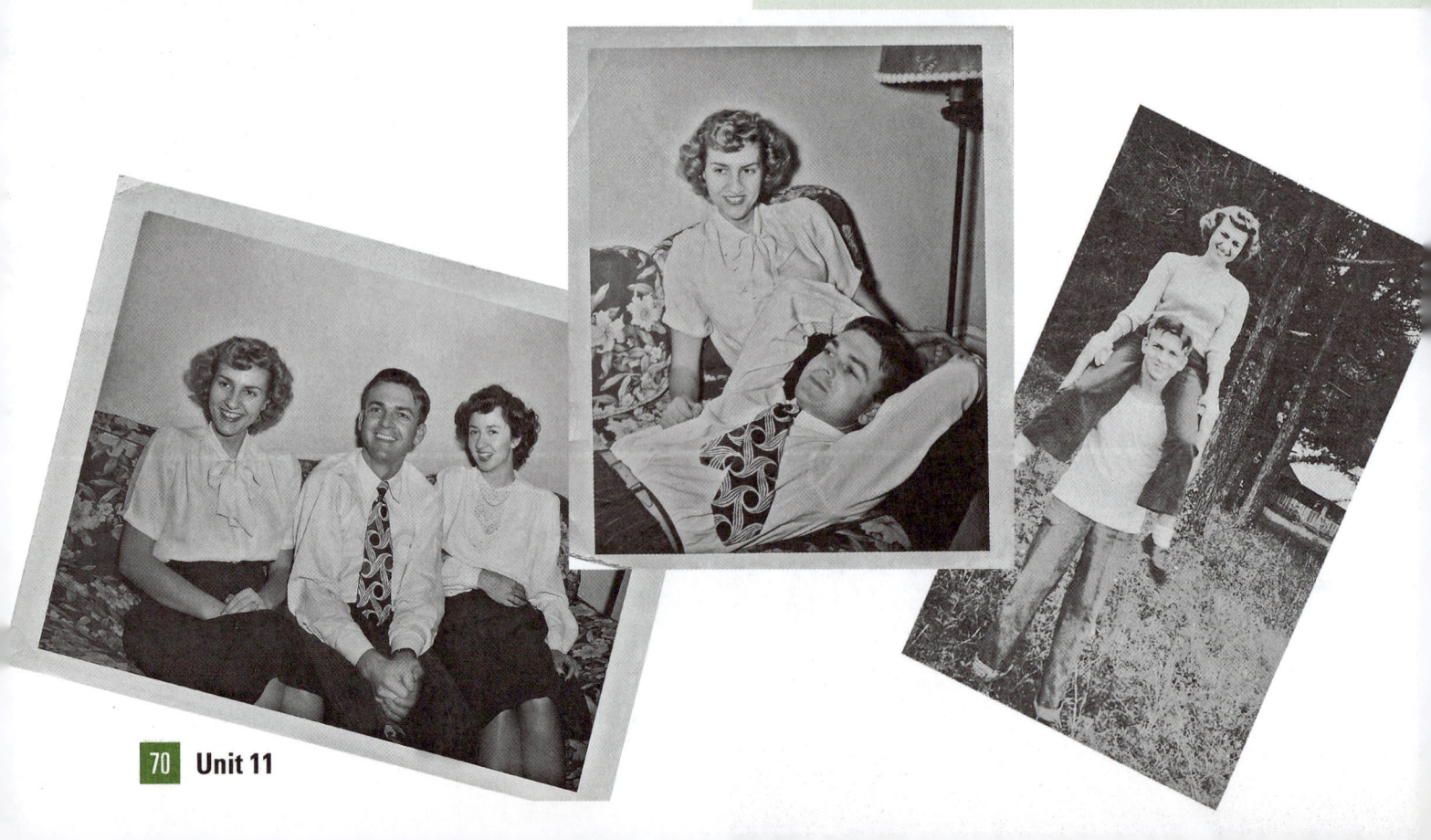

70 Unit 11

B Sean O'Hagan, photography critic

Though I write about photography for a living and have taken many photos in my time, I did not own a camera until a few years ago. Now I try not to shoot as freely as I used to because so many photographers have told me that the real editing takes place as you are shooting. My photos are all saved on my hard disk and this fills me with a vague anxiety. Looking at these photos, I can see that I shoot certain things over and over: landscapes whizzing by from moving trains; people dozing on the tube. I think photographs should be intimate. And everyday. And luminous. When my father was ill a few years ago, I photographed the interior of his garden shed. The images feel like a portrait of him somehow – a portrait of the inside of his head and all the stuff he had collected there. For me, they possess a meaning that many of my other photographs do not.

C Mary McCartney, photographer

My mum was a photographer and I grew up in that world, so I assumed everyone could take pictures. Now I realise that not everyone has the eye. It takes skill, time and attention to do a proper shoot, or go into depth. I'm embarrassed to say that I often tend to take photos on my mobile phone. I like how immediate it is – I can upload images straight onto the web. I upload with filters; I'm not that purist about it. But if there's absolutely stunning light, and a picture hasn't needed a filter, then I'll upload it just as it is. Family pictures are the most precious. I have a set of prints I carry around in my wallet of my kids, my husband and my parents. I look at those rather than writing a diary: they're wonderfully evocative and textural. I change them every so often after they get worn out.

D Blake Morrison, author

My father was scrupulous about documenting his children's childhood, first in tiny black-and-white prints, then with colour transparencies, which were looked at through a viewfinder on a white screen. He also had a cine camera. Why my wife and I never bought a video camera, I don't know (laziness? expense?). Most of my father's snaps, however, were taken without us noticing. But a few were trick photos, such as the one with my mother, sister and me arranged above each other on a steep hill to look like acrobats standing on each other's shoulders. Despite their playfulness, my chief feeling when I look at those photos is sadness: that the times they commemorate can't be retrieved. It's sentimental, I know: time passes; the moment goes as the shutter clicks.

Vocabulary

Three-part phrasal verbs

1 Choose the correct verb in sentences a–h to make three-part phrasal verbs.

a We should *look/take/go* up to the older generation – they have so much wisdom.
b I'm afraid the job didn't *pull/live/move* up to my expectations so I decided to hand in my notice.
c Dad will just have to *look/face/sit* up to the fact that he's not as young as he used to be.
d The only way to deal with bullies is either to run away or *stand/push/call* up to them.
e No one *saw/felt/went* up to going to the concert so we stayed at home instead.
f Thanks for the lovely lunch. It's great to see you, but I'm afraid I've got to *get/take/move* back to work. Bye!
g There was so much to do in the week *going/leading/walking* up to the holiday, that we were exhausted when we finally got on the plane.
h Why don't you *start/wake/jump* up to the fact that you will never pass your exams if you go out all the time?

2 Match phrasal verbs from 1 with meanings 1–8.

1 respect
2 have the energy to do something
3 return
4 confront someone
5 approach or prepare for something
6 accept and deal with something
7 be as good as expected
8 become aware of a situation

3 Make two three-part phrasal verbs from each of 1–3 below.

1	put	down	with
		up	to
2	get	down	with
	come	away	
3	drop	in	of
		out	on

4 Use a dictionary to answer the following questions about the phrasal verbs in 3.

a In which phrasal verb is the object placed before the particles?
b Where is the object of three-part phrasal verbs usually placed?
c What other three-part phrasal verbs can you find for those in 3? What do they mean?

5 Use the phrasal verbs from 3 to replace the words in italics in a–f.

a We don't *tolerate* that kind of behaviour in this school.
b Not many people went to the exhibition. I think this *is because of* the location – it's really hard to find that gallery.
c In winter many elderly people *become ill with* the flu.
d How did Bob manage to *go unpunished for* forgetting his wedding anniversary?
e Almost half of the students *chose to stop going to* the debating society meetings.
f I'm just going to *quickly visit* Jill for a coffee – do you want to come along?

Unit 11

Grammar

Comparatives and superlatives

1 Correct the mistakes with comparatives and superlatives in sentences a–f.

a Have you read his latest novel? It's so boring and just as all the others.
b Sarah hated travelling by coach. In her opinion, it was by far the worse choice. The train was simply the best option.
c She's a lot as her sister. They're both extremely creative and have fiery tempers.
d The more time I spend travelling, the little I want to settle down in one place.
e Why don't we go to the modern art gallery on Thornton Street? It's far interesting than the other one.
f I've never had such a boring holiday. It was not near as good as I thought it would be.

2 Complete sentences a–h using the words below.

> just   no more   nothing   nowhere   great
> bit   nearly   slightly

a Booking online is only .... cheaper than booking by phone.
b According to the airlines, air travel is .... as safe as any other form of transport.
c Season tickets aren't .... as expensive as those bought on a daily basis.
d Buying decent quality sportswear is .... expensive than buying clothes with a designer label.
e Unfortunately, the band's latest album is .... near as good as their previous one.
f Learning to play the piano is .... like as difficult as learning to play the violin.
g If you worked a .... harder, you might actually achieve your objectives.
h Travelling alone is a .... deal more exciting than travelling in a group.

3 Choose four of the expressions in 2 and use them in sentences to compare
- watching DVDs or going to the cinema.
- reading a play or going to the theatre.
- modern art and Renaissance art.

Grammar Extra

so and *such*

4 Complete sentences a–g using *so* or *such*.

a Fresh vegetables, ... as cauliflowers and aubergines, are available at the market.
b The measures have been introduced .... that safety standards can be improved.
c We consider ourselves fortunate to have .... friendly neighbours.
d Housing is expensive in the capital and .... is the cost of parking.
e 'Is Mike here yet?' 'Yes, I think ....'
f It was .... a complicated form that no one could understand how to fill it in.
g Fifty or .... people attended the lecture.

5 Match the examples of *so* and *such* in 4 with uses 1–6 below.

1 to give an example
2 to indicate that something is not exact
3 to say that something else is true
4 to emphasise
5 to offer an explanation
6 to avoid repeating a phrase

Unit 11

Listening

Part 2 Sentence completion

1 Which of the following do you think is necessary to show that you appreciate modern art?

- having a thorough knowledge of art
- obtaining a qualification in art
- creating your own works of art
- behaving in a certain manner at galleries
- owning works by famous artists

2 🎧 You will hear an expert giving some advice on art appreciation. For questions 1-8, complete the sentences.

how to appreciate modern art

Remember that modern art began around the year (1) ....

The aim of modern art was to rebel against (2) ....

It is essential to (3) .... at a gallery.

You need to wear (4) .... during your visit.

Never stand where the (5) .... interfere with your appreciation of a painting.

Remember that (6) .... is taken extremely seriously in galleries.

You can actually get a better view by (7) .... and using binoculars.

Make sure you only stop to look at (8) .... works of art.

Unit 11

Use of English

Part 2 Open cloze

1 Quickly read the text below. What is so unusual about the paintings mentioned in the text?

2 For questions 1–8, read the text again and think of the word which best fits each gap.

Collection of Dalí paintings go on sale

At a glance they seem (0) ...**like**... familiar 19th-century botanical lithographs, the type you see on endless hotel room walls. But look closer and the plum seems to be running away and the raspberries appear embarrassed. The fourteen original watercolour fruit studies were (1) .... fact painted by the surrealist artist Salvador Dalí and are remarkable because they have remained (2) .... or less hidden since 1969, the year of their creation. 'They are wonderful,' said William O'Reilley, director of impressionist and modern art at Bonhams, the auction house that announced their sale (3) .... the hammer.

They were commissioned by the publisher Jean-Paul Schneider and became a series of lithographs. The publisher kept the originals (4) .... their sale to an unnamed European collector. '(5) .... except the buyer had seen the originals since then,' said O'Reilley, who recalled the thrill of entering the seller's house 'and (6) .... they were – on the wall. It was completely unexpected.' The works have names (7) .... as Hasty Plum and Raspberry Blush. Each painting is valued (8) .... £40,000–£70,000.

Part 4 Key word transformation

3 Rewrite the second sentence in a–d keeping the meaning the same. Use three to six words including the word given.

a I want to know if you have finalised those delivery dates yet.
   ROUND
   Have you .... those delivery dates yet?

b Unfortunately, if there is a rise in interest rates, we shall have to increase our prices.
   EVENT
   Unfortunately, ... a rise in interest rates, we shall have to increase our prices.

c Somehow no one found out that he had stolen the technical design from another company.
   GET
   Somehow he managed .... stealing the technical design from another company.

d My best friend became a big name on the stage after leaving drama school.
   WENT
   After leaving drama school my best friend .... a big name on the stage.

Unit 11

A changing world

Reading Part 8 Multiple matching

1 Read the article about how to be environmentally friendly. Which summary of the writer's comments (a–c) is the most accurate?

   a   There are numerous ways to help the planet.
   b   It is pointless to try to follow schemes and ideas.
   c   We should be aware of unexpected consequences of our actions.

2 Read the article again. In which paragraph (A–E) of the text are 1–10 mentioned? The paragraphs may be chosen more than once.

a controversial pastime that raises considerable money	1 …
an action which creates a different weather pattern	2 …
an undesirable result of unnecessary global transportation	3 … 4 …
inadequate research into harmful substances	5 …
people at the greatest risk from factors beyond their control	6 …
a far-reaching change in official attitude	7 …
benefits for those the scheme was not originally intended for	8 … 9 …
the bringing of a source of energy to remote areas	10 …

But will it save the planet?

Unit 12

A Fair trade

Farmers in developing countries are some of the most vulnerable people on earth, prey to world commodity markets, middle men and the weather. So-called 'fair-trade' arrangements guarantee co-operative groups a price above the world market and a bonus on top. The growing fair-trade market has distributed hundreds of millions of pounds to more than 50 million people worldwide. But critics say that fair trade will never lift a country out of poverty; indeed, it may keep it there, because the money generated from sales goes almost in its entirety to rich countries which promote the products. As a simple guide, only about 5% of the sale price of a fair-trade chocolate bar may actually go to the poor country.

B Organic food

For food to be organic it must be free of added chemicals, both in the growing of the food and in the killing of the pests that might damage the crop. In a world where many manufactured chemicals have never been properly tested for safety, this is a very big selling point. Parents are thus prepared to pay a premium for organic food, especially when chemicals suspected of causing a variety of problems have been found, albeit in tiny quantities, in most children's blood. The problem is that many farmers have not switched to organic in sufficient numbers to satisfy this growing market. As a result, supermarkets are often forced to fly 'organic' vegetables halfway round the world, at a great cost to the planet in extra greenhouse gases. Environmentalists are now urging shoppers to buy locally produced vegetables, even if they are not organic.

C Recycling

A great shift has taken place in the way we think about rubbish. Where once we were happy to bury it in landfills, we are now being urged by national and local governments to recycle it and think of waste as a resource. The wheelie-bin culture is being replaced by a series of kerbside collections for paper, metals, plastic, bottles, clothes and compost. The idea is to cut landfill as well as saving the planet. It is, however, having some unexpected consequences. Most of Britain's plastic and paper is now being sent for recycling in China or India, which creates more greenhouse gases just to get it there, plus workers then have to separate it. Meanwhile, some paper and bottles carefully sorted out by householders end up being dumped in landfills after all, because the demand for recycled materials constantly fluctuates.

D Being carbon neutral

If you want to make yourself feel better about the planet, there are lots of ways for you to ease your conscience by becoming 'carbon neutral'. One of the most appealing methods is to pay for someone to plant trees, preferably creating or regenerating new forests. The theory is that trees grow by absorbing carbon dioxide and giving out oxygen, storing the carbon in their trunks. But woods and forests create their own mini-climate, which collects and stores water and creates rainclouds. Added to this, there is the potential problem that planting trees often releases carbon stored in the soil – and what happens if the forests catch fire, or are chopped down and harvested for timber? A better solution might be to invest in small-scale hydro-electric schemes, so that people who live in the Himalayas, for example, and currently do not have electricity, can develop a 21st century lifestyle without polluting the planet.

E Eco-tourism

The idea of 'green' tourism is to persuade local people not to chop down forests or wipe out tigers, but to preserve them so rich tourists visit and peer at the wildlife through binoculars. Unfortunately, the best money is made from reintroducing animals for trophy hunting by the very rich – an idea which does not always meet with approval and has caused much debate. While tourists may help sustain some national parks, they often create as many problems as they solve. One is that they tend to demand all mod cons in their hotels, such as a great deal of water for showers; a luxury sometimes not available for locals. Eco-tourism, when properly managed, can offer the locals and the animals a brighter future. Sometimes, though, the only winners are the hotel owners.

Vocabulary

Meanings of *set*

1 Choose the correct meaning (A–C) of the verb *set* in 1–8.

1 Diana's birthday present was a ruby *set* in a gold ring.
  A organised   B positioned   C marked
2 A deadline for the assignment has not yet been *set*.
  A decided   B regulated   C concluded
3 All questions for the quiz are *set* by experts in their field.
  A studied   B published   C written
4 Leave twenty-four hours for the glue to *set*.
  A harden   B soften   C widen
5 Howard's latest film is *set* in an indeterminate time in the future.
  A comes about   B goes on   C takes place
6 The waitress *set* the dining tables using the best cutlery and crockery.
  A prepared   B placed   C piled
7 Some schools *set* extremely high standards for their students.
  A insert   B expect   C present
8 Our teacher's friendly manner always *set* the tone for her classes.
  A established   B arranged   C insisted

2 Match phrases a–e with 1–5, joining them with the verb *set* in the correct form.

a The writer explained that he …
b To make sure the jelly …
c Since its creation five years ago, the school …
d The company always …
e Unfortunately the date for the reunion …

1 high standards for its teachers.
2 early enough to obtain the preferred venue.
3 job applicants an intelligence test.
4 you need to put it in a cool place.
5 his latest novel in France because he had lived there as a child.

Words with similar meanings

3 Complete sentences a and b with the correct form of the words in 1–4. Use a dictionary to help you.

1 refuse/decline
  a We have to .... your invitation to the opening as we have a prior engagement.
  b Paul .... to admit that he had been the one to cause the accident.
2 refute/reject
  a Despite several job offers, Julia .... them and went back to university.
  b Many people have tried to .... the scientist's theories.
3 deny/disallow
  a The accused .... being anywhere near the scene of the crime.
  b There were numerous objections from the players when the goal was ....
4 resist/oppose
  a The local residents will .... the idea of a new nuclear power plant.
  b I have .... the temptation to open this packet of chocolate biscuits!

4 Read sentences a–e below and explain the meaning of the words in italics. Use a dictionary to check how accurate your answers are.

a Could passengers please *ensure* they have all their belongings with them before leaving the aircraft?
b All doors and windows must be *secured* when the building is vacated.
c I was *assured* that the tickets would be delivered on Monday.
d We strongly advise customers to *insure* their possessions when travelling.
e The purpose of this form is to *ascertain* whether you are eligible for the loan you have requested.

Grammar

Emphasis

1 Match a–g with 1–7 to make complete sentences.

a In no way …
b Only when …
c Little …
d Scarcely …
e No sooner …
f Under no circumstances …
g Nowhere …

1 had the boat left the quay than a storm blew up.
2 we opened the front door did we realise that we had been burgled.
3 had the lead marathon runner reached the finishing line when she collapsed.
4 is this newspaper report a true representation of what actually happened.
5 in the city do staff treat you better than in this hotel.
6 did William suspect what lay in store for him.
7 will I ever speak to him again.

2 Rewrite the following sentences using one of the openers a–g in 1. More than one answer may be possible.

a I have absolutely no intention of resigning.
b They had just finished eating when the doorbell rang.
c We had no idea that we were living next to a notorious criminal.
d I can't find a copy of that book anywhere.
e I decided to buy the car when I saw how cheap it was.

Grammar Extra

too and *enough*

3 Rewrite these sentences using the words in brackets.

Example

The sea isn't warm enough for us to go swimming. (too).
The sea is too cold for us to go swimming.

a Pat is too short to be a professional dancer. (enough) ....
b There aren't enough people using public transport nowadays. (far too) ....
c The training course is too expensive for most people to consider enrolling. (enough) ....
d I'm not old enough to drive. (too) ....
e He spoke too quickly for me to hear what he said. (enough) ....

4 Insert *too* or *enough* in the correct place in sentences a–h.

a If the tea is not hot, I can make you another cup.
b I'm young to vote in an election this year, but next year I'll be able to.
c There's much poverty in the world today.
d Is there time to look at the shops before we check in?
e Didn't you find that documentary far complicated?
f I'm afraid you are just not studying hard this term.
g Have you really got experience to apply for the job?
h Please speak clearly for everyone to hear you.

Listening Part 4 Multiple matching

1 What are the main environmental concerns in your country?

2 🎧 Listen to five people talking about environmental issues and complete the exam task below.

For 1–5, choose from A–H what the people would like governments to do.

A take action now without having to explain their decisions
B provide more funding for thorough scientific studies
C make sure the information they base decisions on is reliable
D pass laws preventing people from harming the environment
E make sure everyone knows the consequences of international travel
F give more individual responsibilities to specific nations
G help poorer nations become more environmentally friendly
H try to get rid of all threats to the environment

Speaker 1 [1]
Speaker 2 [2]
Speaker 3 [3]
Speaker 4 [4]
Speaker 5 [5]

For 6–10, choose from A–H why the people would like governments to do these things.

A to encourage more students to consider science as a career
B to highlight the harm caused by people's ways of living
C to try to limit the amount of climate change already taking place
D to utilise all available natural resources on the planet
E to find answers to questions we cannot answer at the moment
F to prevent developing nations making mistakes made by other nations
G to avoid making decisions which could have damaging financial results
H to increase the production of cheap types of fuel

Speaker 1 [6]
Speaker 2 [7]
Speaker 3 [8]
Speaker 4 [9]
Speaker 5 [10]

80 Unit 12

Use of English

Part 1 Multiple-choice cloze

1 Quickly read the text below about plastic bags, ignoring the gaps, and decide who might have written such a text and why.

2 For questions 1–8, read the text again and decide which answer (A, B, C or D) best fits each gap.

SAY 'NO' TO PLASTIC BAGS

Did you know that on (0) ...A... we take home 150 plastic bags annually? In other words, that's one million plastic bags every minute. This is a truly shocking statistic.

Plastic bags cannot simply be (1) .... of along with your domestic rubbish – they can blow off landfill sites and become highly (2) .... litter which can remain in the environment for years. They are not only an eyesore but a (3) .... to the environment too. For example, plastic bags almost dammed the Buriganga river in Bangladesh, and they are widely (4) .... responsible for causing devastating floods there on two separate (5) ....

They also (6) .... a particular threat to wildlife. More and more dead turtles and whales are discovered washed up on beaches after swallowing plastic bags. To marine life, a plastic bag closely (7) .... a jellyfish.

These are the (8) .... why you should reuse plastic bags or take a small rucksack on trips to the supermarket. Why not take this small step to show that you care about the environment?

0	A average	B normal	C example	D ratio
1	A finished	B thrown	C disposed	D used
2	A evident	B visible	C observable	D marked
3	A risk	B danger	C difficulty	D problem
4	A shown	B taken	C made	D held
5	A occasions	B events	C incidents	D episodes
6	A place	B set	C pose	D generate
7	A resembles	B reminds	C equates	D appears
8	A motives	B reasons	C explanations	D causes

Review Units 10–12

1 Rewrite the second sentence in a–c keeping the meaning the same. Use between three to six words including the word given.

a The Mediterranean is warm, whereas the North Sea is much colder.
   NOTHING
   The North Sea is .... the Mediterranean.

b Tom used to trust Jane, but there's no way he'll ever do that again.
   CIRCUMSTANCES
   Tom used to trust Jane, but .... he ever trust her again.

c I would like to be able to speak Chinese.
   HAD
   I wish I .... to speak Chinese.

2 Write two comparative sentences for each pair of sentences in a–d. Use the words in brackets.

Example
Brass is cheap. Gold is expensive. (nowhere near)
Brass is nowhere near as expensive as gold. Gold is nowhere near as cheap as brass.

a Mexican food is spicy. British food is bland. (far)
b Summer temperatures in France are around 26°C. Summer temperatures in Britain are around 24°C. (only slightly)
c Extreme sports are exciting. Racket sports are boring. (a great deal)
d This exercise is quite difficult. The other exercises are less difficult. (a bit)

3 Put the words in sentences a–e into the correct order. Start with the word in bold.

a long brilliant far was film too **The** but
b allowed **Do** project we to time finish you think enough the have?
c carefully this through haven't enough **We** thought problem
d much has money **The** venture invested company too in already this new
e too application **I'm** arrived be late your for to considered afraid you

4 Complete the paragraph about money with the words below.

■ cash   fares   salary   money   change
   wages   bills

There is a saying '1 .... makes the world go round' but whether this is true or not is debatable. What is perhaps true is that our style of living is dictated not by the amount of small 2 .... we have in our pocket but by our annual 3 .... , or the 4 .... we manage to earn on a regular basis. Without those, we wouldn't be able to pay the 5 .... , or afford the 6 .... to get us to work. And if we have nothing in the bank, the 7 .... dispenser is of little use.

5 Combine the two sentences in a–f beginning with the words given.

a James finished cooking dinner. His sister arrived.
   No sooner ....

b He overheard my phonecall to the bank. I didn't know this.
   Little ....

c The plane landed on the narrow runway. All the passengers began to cheer.
   Scarcely ....

d Central Park is beautiful. You won't find a park like this anywhere else in the city.
   Nowhere ....

e There was a cry of protest from the audience. The politician mentioned taxes.
   Only when ....

f I reached home. The heavens opened.
   Hardly ....

82 Review Units 10–12

6 Complete the three-part phrasal verbs in a–g.

a Much to my disappointment, studying abroad didn't .... my expectations.
b I don't really .... going out this evening, I'm afraid.
c I don't know how Anne has .... that dreadful boyfriend of hers for so long.
d Unfortunately, the children have .... chicken pox.
e Do .... us for a coffee if you have a few minutes spare tomorrow. We'll be at home all day.
f I .... his disgraceful behaviour .... the fact that he was exhausted after the long journey.
g I've .... a great idea for the end of term party. I think you'll like it.

7 Put the verbs in brackets into the correct form to make suitable conditional sentences.

a Tim often wishes he .... (join) the navy instead of going to work in a bank.
b As long as you .... (not/make a noise), you can watch the film.
c If only the children .... (stop) making so much mess!
d Supposing I .... (tell) you the truth – do you think you would have believed me?
e If I .... (not/drive) so fast the accident might never have happened!
f The meeting will take place unless something unforeseen .... (happen).

8 Write a synonym or explanation for each expression with *set*.

a My sister got a beautiful ring for her birthday – it's a ruby *set* in pearls.
b I'm reading a fascinating novel which is *set* in the eighteenth century.
c The team *sets* high standards for its existing and potential members.
d We haven't *set* a date for our holiday, but it will probably be sometime in June.
e If you don't put the mousse in the fridge, it won't *set*.

9 Complete sentences a–g with *so* or *such*.

a 'Is there any coffee left in the cupboard?' 'I don't think ....'
b The restaurant, ... as it was, closed down last month.
c It was .... an easy exam that I'm sure I've passed!
d Bill reached for a glass on the top shelf. As he did .... , he knocked over a vase.
e My best friend's just bought a new mobile phone. And .... have I.
f We went on holiday out of season .... we could save some money.
g This is .... a complicated instruction manual that I can't understand anything.

10 Choose the correct word to complete sentences a–h.

a The company's representative *denied/refused* to comment on the allegations of fraud.
b Please *ensure/assure* that you switch off your car alarm before leaving your vehicle.
c The results of the research were *declined/refuted* by experts in the medical field.
d Investigators are still trying to *assure/ascertain* the cause of the plane crash.
e The children *denied/rejected* all knowledge of the broken window.
f Ron *secured/assured* his boss that he would do his best to meet the deadline.
g I will do everything in my power to *oppose/resist* the proposed new law.
h It really is very important that you *ensure/insure* your belongings.

Review Units 10–12 83

Writing

This writing section contains twelve practice tasks for Paper 2 of the Cambridge English: Advanced exam.

Each task practises the same task presented in the Student's Book and, in most cases, shares the same topic.

For help with the tasks, look back at the Student's Book and refer to the:
- **Writing** section and how to do it boxes in the corresponding unit
- **Writing Guide** on pages 154–165 for model answers and phrase banks

The **Vocabulary** and **Grammar** sections in the Student's Book and the Workbook will help you use a broad range of structures and vocabulary.

Write your answers in **220–260 words** in an appropriate style.

Unit 1   Part 2 A formal letter

Your friend is applying for the job below and has asked you to write a letter giving him/her a character reference explaining why he/she would be a suitable candidate for the job.

Social Programme Organiser

A well-established language school for international students is looking for someone to organise and run a social programme for students during their free time. If you are:

- energetic
- resourceful
- organised

you are the person we need.

Write your **letter**.

Unit 2 Part 2 A proposal

You are on a committee planning a festival in your town. You have been asked to write a proposal suggesting what could be included in the festival. Your proposal should outline:

- what should be included to best represent your town.
- why your suggestions would appeal to local people.
- what might be included to attract visitors from elsewhere.

Write your **proposal**.

Unit 3 Part 1 An essay

You have read a book on what life might be like in the future. You have made the notes below.

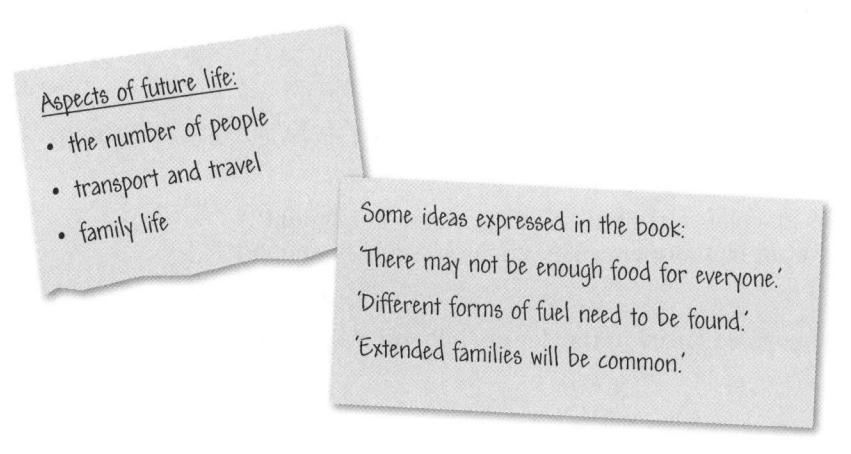

Aspects of future life:
- the number of people
- transport and travel
- family life

Some ideas expressed in the book:
'There may not be enough food for everyone.'
'Different forms of fuel need to be found.'
'Extended families will be common.'

Write an essay discussing **two** of the aspects of life mentioned in your notes. You should **explain how you think these aspects might change in the future, giving reasons** in support of your opinion.

You may, if you wish, make use of the ideas expressed in the book, but you should use your own words as far as possible.

Unit 4 Part 2 A report

An international organisation called Back to Nature has asked you to write a report on how people can appreciate the countryside near where you live.

You should include details of interesting places, what these places have to offer and what steps have been taken to encourage people to visit these places responsibly.

Write your **report**.

Unit 5 Part 1 An essay

Your class has had a debate on how to encourage young people to lead healthier lifestyles. You have made the notes below.

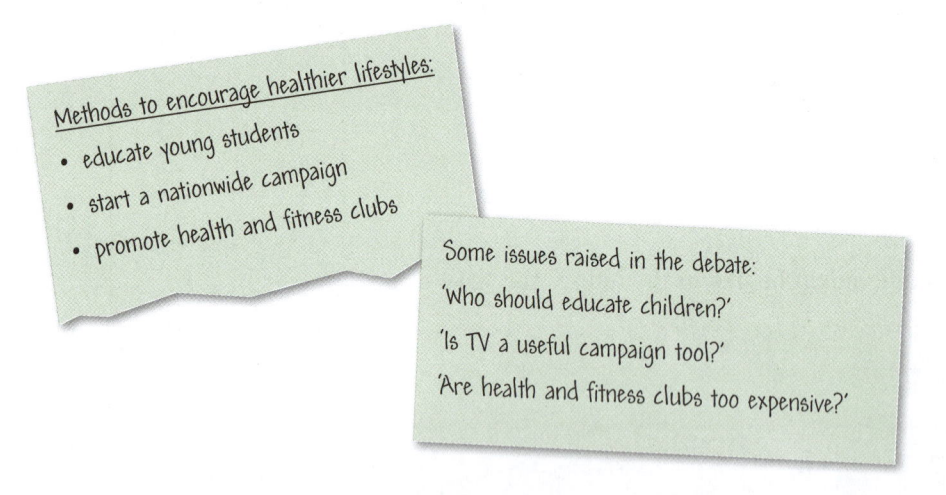

Methods to encourage healthier lifestyles:
- educate young students
- start a nationwide campaign
- promote health and fitness clubs

Some issues raised in the debate:
'Who should educate children?'
'Is TV a useful campaign tool?'
'Are health and fitness clubs too expensive?'

Write an essay discussing **two** of the strategies mentioned in your notes. You should **explain which strategy you think would be more effective, giving reasons** in support of your opinion.

You may, if you wish, make use of the issues raised in the debate, but you should use your own words as far as possible.

Unit 6   Part 2 A review

You see this advertisement in a magazine for young people.

> **Reviews wanted**
>
> We want to encourage young people to read more. Help us do this by sending us a review which describes two of the best books you have ever read. Make sure you give reasons for your choices.

Write your **review**.

Unit 7   Part 2 A proposal

You are on a planning committee organising an exhibition of the history of the area where you live. You have been asked to write a proposal suggesting what should appear in the exhibition so that the committee can make a decision about what form the exhibition should take. Your proposal should outline what aspects of local history should be included in the exhibition and how these aspects could be presented.

Write your **proposal**.

Unit 8   Part 2 An informal email

You recently did some volunteer work for a charity that raises money to help people in need. You have received an email from a friend asking whether you would recommend that he/she does some similar volunteer work during the summer holidays. Reply to your friend's email. You should include:

- your reactions to your own volunteer experience.
- whether you would recommend volunteer work to your friend or not.
- your reasons for your opinions.

Write your **email**.

Unit 9 Part 1 An essay

Your class has had a class discussion on crime prevention. You have made the notes below.

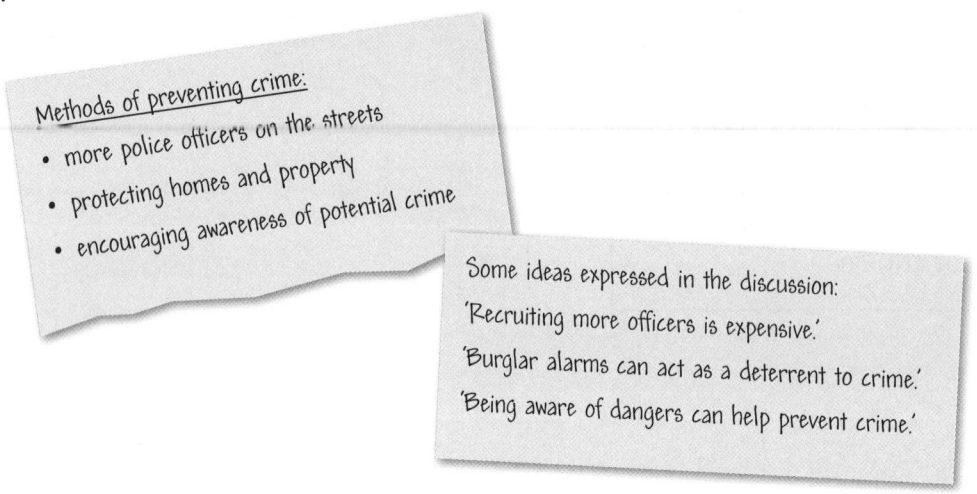

Methods of preventing crime:
- more police officers on the streets
- protecting homes and property
- encouraging awareness of potential crime

Some ideas expressed in the discussion:
'Recruiting more officers is expensive.'
'Burglar alarms can act as a deterrent to crime.'
'Being aware of dangers can help prevent crime.'

Write an essay discussing **two** of the methods mentioned in your notes. You should **explain which method you think is more effective, giving reasons** in support of your opinion.

You may, if you wish, make use of the ideas expressed in the discussion, but you should use your own words as far as possible.

Unit 10 Part 2 A report

The International Recruiting Agency has asked you to write a report on the employment of young people in your country.

Your report should explain which jobs are currently most popular with young people in your country, why these jobs are popular with that age group and what companies can do to make jobs more attractive to young people.

Write your **report**.

Unit 11 Part 2 A review

You see this announcement in an international magazine called *The World of Television*.

> **The best entertainment for all**
>
> We believe television is for everybody. That's why we want you to write us a review recommending two television programmes in your country – one for teenagers and the other for an older age group.
>
> Your review should describe one programme for each group, commenting on the style and content of each programme and explaining why it is suitable for that age group.

Write your **review**.

Unit 12 Part 1 An essay

You have just listened to a talk on how the world is changing. You have made the notes below.

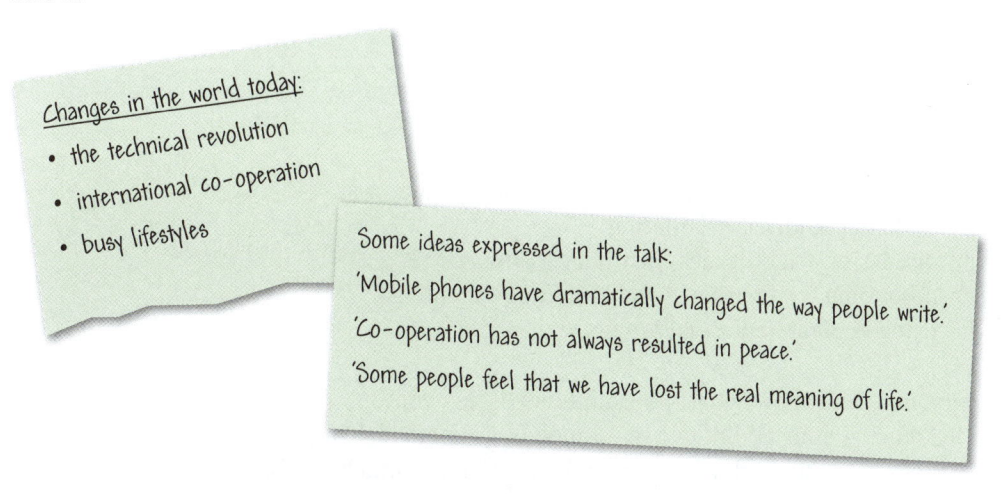

Changes in the world today:
- the technical revolution
- international co-operation
- busy lifestyles

Some ideas expressed in the talk:
'Mobile phones have dramatically changed the way people write.'
'Co-operation has not always resulted in peace.'
'Some people feel that we have lost the real meaning of life.'

Write an essay discussing **two** of the changes mentioned in your notes. You should **explain whether these changes are positive or negative, giving reasons** in support of your opinion.

You may, if you wish, make use of the ideas expressed in the talk, but you should use your own words as far as possible.

Speaking

This speaking section contains practice activities for Paper 4 of the Cambridge English: Advanced exam. Some of the tasks, tips and photos are taken from the Student's Book, and there are some additional tasks.

For help with the tasks, look back at the Student's Book and refer to the Speaking section and *How to do it* boxes in each unit.

Remember, too, that the Vocabulary and Grammar sections in the Student's Book and Workbook will help you improve your language skills and extend your vocabulary. This, in turn, will help you to give better responses in the Speaking paper.

Quick quiz

Read the information about the Speaking paper on page 8 of the Student's Book and answer these questions.

1 How long is the Speaking paper? .... minutes

2 Which parts of the Speaking paper are being described in a–d?
   a Talk on your own using visual and written prompts. Part ....
   b Discuss a problem-solving task using written prompts. Part ....
   c Answer questions about yourself. Part ....
   d Talk about discussion points related to the previous section. Part ....

3 Match each of the parts of the Speaking paper to the abilities they test.
   Part 1 .... a exchanging ideas, negotiating
   Part 2 .... b discussing wider issues, justifying opinions
   Part 3 .... c describing, comparing, speculating, commenting
   Part 4 .... d using general and social language

4 Complete the gaps in a–e to show what the examiners assess you on.
   a G............. Resource – your ability to use a range of grammatical structures accurately.
   b L............. R............. – your ability to use a range of appropriate vocabulary.
   c D............. M............. – your ability to state your ideas clearly and without hesitation.
   d P............. – your ability to produce individual sounds correctly and use appropriate stress and intonation.
   e I............. C............. – your ability to initiate, respond and develop interaction with other speakers.

Part 1

1 Which of these questions or statements would you expect to hear in Part 1?
a Where are you from?
b Which activity in the pictures do you think is most useful?
c How long have you been studying English?
d What kind of work would you like to do in the future?
e Now you have a minute to decide what would be the best way to make important decisions.
f What sorts of books or magazines do you like to read?

2 Use these words to complete the *How to do it* tips below.

expand   one   interrupt   eye contact   appropriate   speak   long

how to do it

1 Use .... tenses to express your ideas.
2 Don't .... your partner when he/she is answering a question.
3 Don't take too .... to reply. Begin speaking immediately.
4 Don't simply give ....word answers.
5 .... on your answers by giving examples.
6 .... clearly enough for both examiners to hear you.
7 Remember to maintain .... with the interlocutor when appropriate.

3 What answers would you give to these questions? Use the useful phrases below and the *How to do it* tips above to help you.
- Do you think you have too much or too little free time? (Why?)
- Would you like to spend time living and working in another country? (Why?)
- What do you think has been your greatest achievement in life so far?
- What kind of job do you hope to do in the future?
- How do you usually travel to school/work?

Answering personal questions
Well, actually …
That's a difficult question, but …
I've never given it much thought but …
As a matter of fact …

Expressing personal views
In my opinion, …
I think it's essential to …
I strongly believe that …
As far as I'm concerned …

Talking about the future
I'm not really sure what …
I wouldn't be surprised if …
I think I'll probably decide to …
I doubt if I'll …
It's unlikely that I'll …

Speaking 91

Part 2

1 Which of these statements about Part 2 are true and which are false?
a You should talk about all three of the pictures you are given.
b There are always two questions printed above each set of photographs.
c You need to compare the pictures, not simply describe them.
d You have time to prepare what you are going to say about your chosen pictures.
e The examiner will stop you when your allotted time has come to an end.
f You will be asked to comment for about one minute on your partner's pictures.

2 This is a transcript of what one student said in response to the first question in the Part 2 task below. Complete the missing words. More than one answer may be possible.

'Well, I think **1** .... of these photos show ceremonies **2** .... would be quite difficult to set up. A graduation ceremony involves a lot of people – you have to invite not only the students who are graduating, but their relatives and guests too. **3** .... addition to this, lots of degree certificates would have to be prepared and printed. On the other **4** .... , this other ceremony – I think it **5** .... be the opening ceremony of the Olympic Games – would be **6** .... more challenging to organise. The people **7** .... participate in an event **8** .... this one come from lots of different countries and **9** .... a result they would all speak different languages.

- How difficult might it be to organise ceremonies like these?
- What might the atmosphere be like at the ceremonies?

3 Work with a partner. Take it in turns to do the Part 2 task above. Choose **two** photos to talk about. You should each speak for about one minute. Use the phrases below to help you and remember to answer both of the questions.

Speculating
It looks like/looks as if it is …
The people seem to be/appear to be …
There might be/could be …

4 Now look at each other's chosen photos and answer the follow-up question. You should each speak for about 30 seconds. Use the phrases below to help you.

Which of these ceremonies do you think would attract the biggest audience? (Why?)

Making decisions and giving reasons
It's difficult to decide between these two, but …
I'd (definitely) go for this one because …
It has to be this one because …

Speaking

Parts 3 and 4

1 Choose the correct option to complete the sentences about Parts 3 and 4.
 a Part 3 is divided into *two/three* sections.
 b Candidates are given *only oral instructions/oral instructions and written prompts* in the first section of Part 3.
 c Candidates have up to *15/30* seconds to look at the first section of the Part 3 task.
 d Candidates have *two/three* minutes to speak in the first section of Part 3.
 e Candidates talk together for *one part/the whole* of Part 3.
 f The examiner *takes/does not take* part in the discussion in Part 3.
 g A conclusion *should/shouldn't* be reached in the first part of Part 3.
 h Candidates *see/don't see* the questions in Part 4.
 i The questions in Part 4 *are/are not* related to the Part 3 discussion.
 j Candidates *should/don't need to* agree on the discussion points in Part 4.

2 Match the two halves of these sentences, which give advice about how to approach Parts 3 and 4.
 a Encourage   1 to repeat if you haven't heard something.
 b Disagree politely   2 for your opinions.
 c Quickly correct   3 with your partner, if you wish.
 d Listen carefully   4 any mistakes you make.
 e Try to give reasons   5 to the questions the examiner asks you.
 f Try to discuss   6 eye-contact with the examiner.
 g Don't maintain   7 all the written prompts.
 h Only ask the examiner   8 your partner to speak.

3 With a partner, do the first section of this Part 3 task. Take about 2 minutes to discuss the question using the prompts provided. Use the phrases at the bottom of the page to help you.

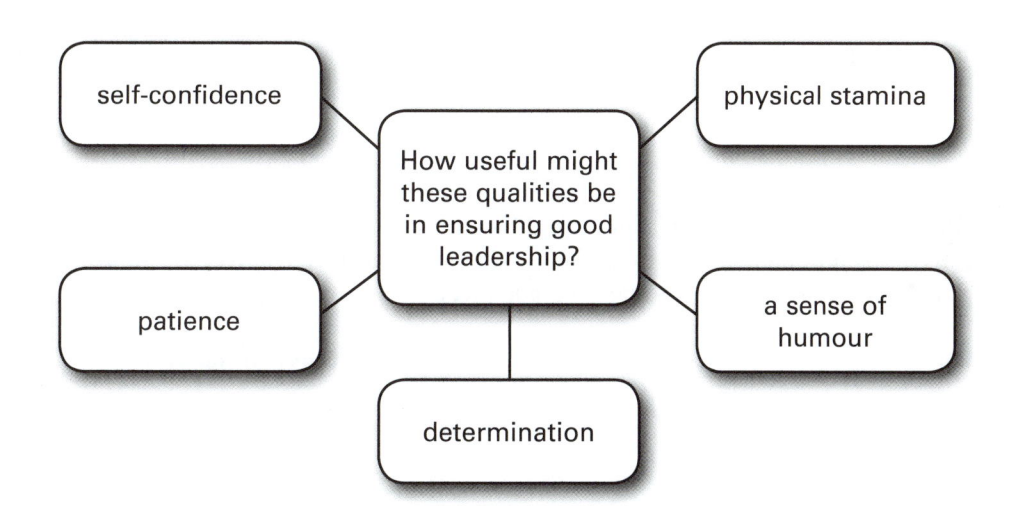

- self-confidence
- physical stamina
- patience
- a sense of humour
- determination

How useful might these qualities be in ensuring good leadership?

Inviting your partner to speak
Do/Don't you think this one ... ?
Personally, I (don't) think this one ... . What about you?
I believe ... , don't you?
Would(n't) you agree that ... ?
What do you think about this one?
How about you, what would you say?
How do you feel about the others?

Suggesting alternatives
You have a point, but ...
That's true, but don't you think that ... ?
I'm not sure if I agree with you. What about ... ?
I can see what you mean, but ...
Yes, but on the other hand ...
I agree with you up to a point, but ...

4 Look at the Part 3 task from page 93 again and do the second section of the task. Take one minute to discuss this question with your partner. Use the phrases below the prompts to help you.

> Which of the qualities would it be most difficult for a good leader to manage without?

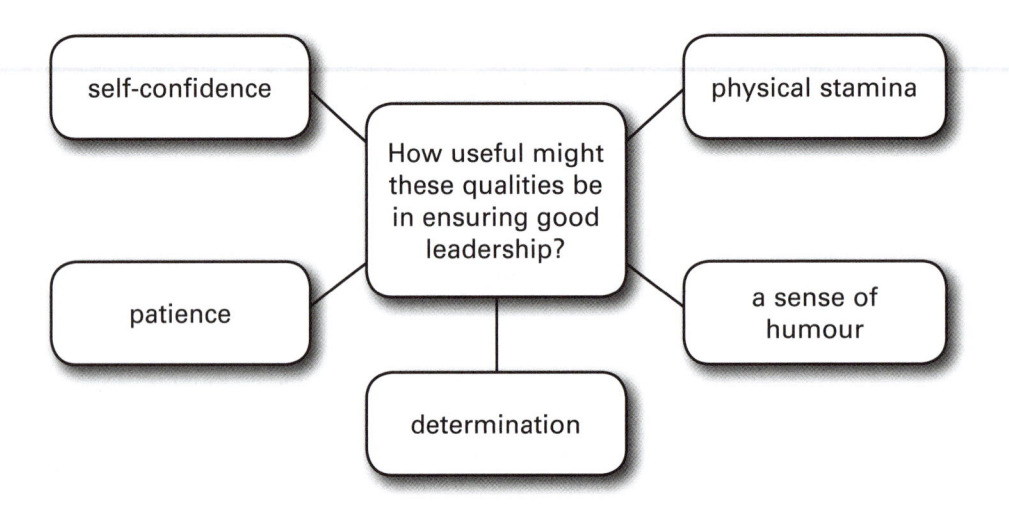

- self-confidence
- physical stamina
- patience
- a sense of humour
- determination

How useful might these qualities be in ensuring good leadership?

Reaching a decision
So, which one do you think is the most/least ... ?
Which of them would you choose?
I really think that this one is ... because ...
I'd definitely select this one because ...
Can you explain why you've suggested that one?
It seems that we both agree that ...
Well, I think ... but you apparently think ... . Let's agree to disagree.

5 With your partner, discuss these Part 4 questions. Use the phrases below to help you.
- Some people say good leaders are born, not made. What's your view?
- Why do you think some leaders end up being very unpopular?
- Do you think it is important what a leader looks like? (Why/Why not?)
- How necessary do you think it is for groups of human beings to have leaders?
- How can schools encourage children to become good leaders?

Expressing opinions
In my opinion ...
From my point of view, ...
I (don't) believe/think ...
I feel strongly that ...
It seems to me that ...
As far as I'm concerned ...
Some people believe ... , but I personally think that ...
It's certainly true that ...

Discussing pros and cons
On the one hand, ... /On the other hand, ...
Although ... , ...
However, ...
Whereas, ...
In addition, ...

Giving examples
For example/instance, ...
One example of ... is ...

Speaking

Key

Unit 1

Reading

1 c

2 1 C 2 B 3 C 4 C 5 A 6 D

Vocabulary

1 Positive: confident, cheerful, optimistic, excited

Negative: depressed, fed up, moody, pessimistic, bored

Neutral: curious, resolute, realistic

a fed up
b pessimistic
c optimistic
d confident
e realistic
f moody
g curious
h excited
i bored

2
a extract or obtain more from
b avoid doing something
c understand
d nearly
e becoming
f have a good relationship
g began
h achieving nothing

3
a get on with
b get down to
c getting us nowhere
d getting on for
e get more out of
f get
g get out of

Grammar

1
1 A: to buy   B: changing
2 A: making   B: spending
3 A: giving   B: seeing
4 A: receiving   B: not informing
5 A: boasting   B: mention
6 A: commuting   B: to look

2
a enter   e to provide
b to accept   f to solve
c to complete   g to strike
d feel   h to inform

3
a 2 for forgetting
b 4 of stealing
c 7 for not panicking
d 1 from smoking
e 3 for not living up to
f 5 from rushing
g 6 of travelling

(*at, on* and *by* are not needed)

Listening

2 1 C   2 D   3 H   4 F   5 G
      6 D   7 A   8 E   9 B   10 H

Audio script

Speaker 1
Last month I arranged to go out with my best friend Jenny. At the last minute she rang to say she wasn't feeling well. As luck would have it, I got an unexpected invitation to a dinner party. Imagine my surprise when I walked in and saw her sitting there, socialising with my hosts. I emailed her the next day asking her why she'd lied. In my opinion friends should put each other before anyone else. She replied saying that she didn't have to explain herself to me because our friendship had 'run its course'. I was devastated because I knew then that she just didn't see me as part of her life any more.

Speaker 2
One day my husband was rushed to hospital in another town for an emergency operation. My best friend was very supportive and offered to help when she could but all the others just said they wouldn't be able to. It was funny but the people I almost admired were those who were prepared to admit that they couldn't help but gave plausible reasons for not being able to do so. I've now come to the conclusion that you can be so-called friends with people for years, but it's all rather superficial. We show other people our lively, desirable selves. So when we suddenly become vulnerable, we turn into people our friends don't recognise.

Speaker 3
I'm one of those guys with a fat address book – maybe because all my friends tell me I'm charming! But as far as I'm concerned, friendship is a club of seven people which was full by the time I was 23. We all share the same interests, and we don't make any demands on one another in emotional terms – which is something I would avoid like the plague. It's not that I don't like making new friends but I just don't need them. We all grew up in the same social, professional and geographical world that we now occupy as adults. The group offers me as much security and intimacy as I require.

Speaker 4
I'm thrilled when I get invitations from new people because you never know who you might meet as a result of them. I make new friends easily but I drop my old ones with equal ease. At the same time, I believe we should be loyal to our friends while we still have them. I think I'm perfectly consistent because in my view, friendships should be automatically dissolved as soon as one participant finds the other boring – from that moment on any demands made on each other should cease. What exasperates me is some people's tendency to keep pursuing me when it's clear the whole thing has come to an end.

Speaker 5
I've been part of a group of friends for quite a few years. Everyone in the group is ambitious and competitive. I can honestly say that my membership of the group has been a greater source of pride to me than my career. But last year I fell out with the most popular couple in the group and gradually, I sensed that my family and I were being excluded from the group's joint activities. I think what hurt me most was the realisation that even within the group I'd thought of as a refuge, your status inside it was all that counted. No one was prepared to alienate the pair who are the 'leaders of the pack'.

Use of English

1 c

2
1 beneficial   5 orally
2 presentation   6 professional
3 noticeable   7 responses
4 speech   8 unease/uneasiness

3
a advice, advisor
b (un)presentable, present/presence/presenter/presentation
c noticeably
d speech, speaker
e professor/professional
f impressionable, unimpressionable
g responsive, unresponsive
h confident, confidential

Unit 2

Reading

1
a The indigenous people of Lapland.
b The separation of the reindeer herds into family groups, according to the signs on the ears of each yearling calf, for the winter grazing.
c He/She was negative about the experience at first, but at the end felt it was a 'privilege'.

2 1 C 2 F 3 E 4 G 5 A 6 D

Vocabulary

1
a imaginative, existing only in the imagination
b exhausting, thorough and detailed
c conscious, doing something thoroughly and carefully
d satisfactory, giving a feeling of pleasure
e sensitive, realistic and practical
f indignant, native, or from a surrounding area

2
a satisfactory   d consciencious
b imaginative   e sensitive
c exhaustive   f indignant

3
a bar   d mark
b picture   e hour
c data
Suggested answers
a handbag, hand baggage, handball, handbell, handcuff
b film-maker, film noir, filmstrip
c news agency, newscaster, newsletter
d sideboard, sidecar, sideline, side order
e workbook, work experience, workforce

4 a 2 b 2/3 c 2/4 d 3 e 1/3/5

5
a turnout   e setback
b takeover   f turnover
c breakthrough   g handover
d handout   h breakout

Grammar

1
1 to going   6 on sending
2 on travelling   7 about/of expanding
3 at coping
4 in wasting   8 in establishing
5 to being

2
a 2 to convince   d 3 driving
b 5 to resign   e 4 to have
c 1 to be doing   f 6 stealing

3 Suggested answers
a This is the old car **in which** William travelled across Europe.
b The new train, **whose** design is certainly innovative, can reach speeds of 300 km per hour.
c The Welsh mountains, **where** I spent most of my childhood, are very beautiful.
d We met other employees, most **of whom** had been with the company for a few years.
e Winning the World Cup was one of those wonderful moments **when** you feel perfectly happy.
f The film star, **who** will be at the premiere in New York tomorrow, is the subject of much gossip.
g We cannot explain **why** the accident happened.

Listening

2 1 B 2 C 3 A 4 B 5 B 6 A

Audio script

Extract one
A: I understand that your series of food guides is written to help tourists abroad find places where they can sample the authentic, traditional food of that country?
B: Essentially you're right. But it's a little more than that. Yes, the guides list particular places to eat but I've also included sections on the history of the dishes too – you know, how all the favourite dishes have developed and why, and also how they've changed over the years.
A: Why do you think tourists need a guide like this?
B: A country's food is part of its identity and a visitor to that country should be able to find places where they can eat what the inhabitants eat and in some places observe the customs associated with meal times. You can't find this in the big hotels and restaurants – everything is adapted to the foreigner's taste! That's why my series focuses on the small, difficult-to-find places that the locals go to. I also think it's interesting to learn something about the history of traditional dishes and, for me, the way table manners differ from country to country is quite fascinating.

Extract two
A: It seems strange but one of the most important moments of my childhood was when I discovered the Tooth Fairy didn't exist!
B: The Tooth Fairy?

96 Key

A: I'm not sure whether this is a British thing or whether other countries have a similar custom. You know, when you're little and your tooth falls out, you put it under your pillow at night and the Tooth Fairy takes it and leaves you some money? Of course, it's your parents really but it's magical for kids.
B: Yes! But you have to be fast asleep in your bed.
A: That's right! My parents were very good at keeping up the custom and for years I believed it. One year, I remember, we were on holiday in Greece and I lost a tooth. I was so worried that the Tooth Fairy didn't work there but she came and left me some money! A few years later, when I found out it had been my mother all along, I was devastated! I've kept up the tradition with my children though because I think these beliefs are a really important part of your childhood.

Extract three
A: Ayers Rock, or Uluru as the Aborigines call it, is situated in the National Park and is run by the local Aborigines. It is the world's largest single block of stone. It's considered one of the great wonders of the world. Depending on the time of day and the weather, the rock can dramatically change colour, and it's a very popular place with artists and tourists alike.
B: And can people climb the rock?
A: It can be climbed but not by outsiders. It's all to do with respecting the Aborigines – they believe that the area around the rock is inhabited by their ancestors. They also think that the rock is hollow underground and that it contains a special energy source. They believe that the path up the rock was the traditional route taken by their ancestors and today it is associated with important ceremonies. They also feel they have a duty to ensure the safety of visitors and would feel terrible if anything happened to a tourist while climbing.

Use of English

1 It started when two high school students made six snow statues in Odori Park in Sapporo.

2
1 itself   5 its
2 at   6 like
3 when   7 then/afterwards
4 later   8 such

3
a are in favour of observing
b accustomed to being invited
c dramatic increase/rise in attendance (figures)
d to put up with
e much higher than it has ever

Unit 3

Reading

1 a D b A, B and C

2 1 A 2 D 3 C 4 C

3 Extract A: a crux b vested interest
Extract B: c malnutrition
           d proceed
Extract C: e cue f meticulously
Extract D: g implications
           h caveats

Vocabulary

1
a cutback 4   c upbringing 2
b downfall 1   d input 5

2 a 2 b 1 c 6 d 5 e 4 f 3

3
a Handing out   d make out
b stand out   e knocked out
c passes out   f turns out

4
a over 2   d in 1
b of 6   e down 5
c away 4   f down 3

Grammar

1
1 will know/find out
2 has met/meets
3 will perform/is performing
4 knows
5 won't affect
6 will sell out/will have sold out
7 will be given
8 will be talking

2
1 a, b, d
2 c, d, e, f

4 **your opinion** fascinating disgusting
size/weight tiny heavy
age young ancient
shape rectangular oval
colour orange purple
country of origin Chinese Russian
material silk china

5
a (On Saturday) spoke (very well) at the conference (on Saturday)
b Christopher probably knows the way to our house. Jill probably doesn't know the way.
c I quite agree with you. I just love your new flat.
d I can see the ship very/pretty clearly on the horizon now.

Listening

2 1 C 2 B 3 D 4 B 5 D 6 A

Audio script

I: Pete and Sally – thanks for coming to talk to us today. Now, you're about to embark on a journey of epic proportions, aren't you? Tell us about it.
P: Well, it's an extremely ambitious project. We're travelling through Siberia, through thousands of miles of uninhabited forest – and in winter! But apparently there are fewer swamps then. And it's obviously going to take us a long time – five months at least. But what really makes it different is that we'll be travelling on two motorbikes.
I: Now all this may sound like quite a challenge to most of our listeners, and I'm sure the question they would all like to ask is why are you doing it?
S: We could just say 'why not?' or 'we were feeling a bit bored and looking for some excitement', but that's not the whole truth. One of our aims is certainly to try and raise some money for our favourite charity. But what's really behind it is that it's always been our dream. And if we make it, and we're still speaking to each other, we might even enter the record books as being the first married couple to complete a journey of this kind and still remain friends!

Key 97

I: Now I know that you've already survived some pretty hazardous conditions on previous trips to Africa and other countries – so how do you feel about what's ahead of you now?
P: Well, there are some stages that are a little alarming to say the least. In fact, it might just prove to be the most perilous journey we've attempted so far. We'll virtually leave civilisation behind to go through some of the most inhospitable terrain in the world. It's a journey that could be full of danger – and who knows what will happen if we break down in the middle of nowhere, especially in such cold conditions.
I: And what do your friends and family make of all this?
S: Those who know something about the terrain we're about to cross have warned us that the journey will be hazardous in winter. There's the wind chill, not to mention the very real threat of freezing to death. It could all be over sooner than we think if we're not careful! I think some of our friends are a bit dubious about our chances because they've read a lot about winter conditions in Siberia – particularly the places we're heading for, so they know how bad it can get. But we're trying to stay positive.
I: So what steps are you taking to try and prevent disasters?
P: Well, we've planned very carefully so that food and other basic supplies will be available en route. In fact, the supply requirement shaped the route itself in detail. We're going to gather enough emergency supplies for up to a week at a time, so we won't starve if we get stranded. And we're enjoying as many hot meals as we can now – just in case we end up having to eat dried food for days, which can get very monotonous. We're also trying to prepare for freezing temperatures. Temperatures in Siberia can fall well below those of the Arctic, so we're very aware that frostbite could be a real concern. Things like wearing inappropriate footwear or not wearing gloves can be fatal in icy conditions. And frostbite can happen very quickly – at anything below zero degrees centigrade. However, the lower the temperature, the quicker the damage occurs, and the wind-chill factor increases the risk. So we've invested in specialist clothing specifically designed for the Arctic. That should keep us from harm in the extreme cold.
I: And how often do you plan to have rest periods on the journey?
S: Well, when you're planning a rest stop, you have to watch the weather conditions. Sometimes, it's actually better to keep going than wait for it to pass. But other times, you've got to accept that you can't go on until the weather improves. Even a few inches of fresh snow can make all the difference when you're riding a motorbike, so we're just going to adjust our plans and be flexible.
I: And when it's all over, when do you hope to be heading home?
P: Not until we've arrived at the most eastern tip of Siberia. After that we'll travel to Hong Kong and fly home from there. But it won't be until we're just about to land at Heathrow that we'll be saying: 'We're home, this is it!'
I: Sally, Pete – good luck and we hope to see you when you're safely back!
S/P: Thank you.

Use of English

2 1 C 2 C 3 A 4 D
   5 B 6 C 7 D 8 B

Review Units 1–3

1 a workshop   e filmscript
   b setback   f side effect
   c breakthrough   g turnout
   d newsagent

2 a stand   d cut
   b turned   e brought
   c knocked   f stand

3 a Tim had an extremely fascinating, rather small …
   b Did you enjoy yourself at the beach yesterday?
   c We found the restaurant pretty easily.
   d What a disgusting old oval wooden table!
   e I just love your new dress.
   f What a dirty, enormous, rectangular pencil case!
   g Brenda quite likes being on her own.

4 a I showed John the photograph.
   b Susie bought her brother a bicycle for his birthday.
   c My new car cost me a fortune!
   d The authorities insisted on seeing Robert's visa.
   e Fetch the visitors some coffee, would you?
   f The principal promised the students an extra day's holiday.
   g My dentist recommended having two wisdom teeth taken out.
   h Be careful not to leave the appliance switched on after using it.

5 a sensitive   d satisfying
   b exhausting   e conscientious
   c imaginary

6 a would prefer it if
   b succeeded in winning
   c we recommend washing

7 a input   d cutbacks
   b outburst   e upbringing
   c downfall

8 a nowhere   d on
   b on   e out
   c down

9 a where   d why
   b whose   e when
   c of whom   f of which

10 1 b 2 c 3 c 4 a 5 a 6 b 7 a

Unit 4

Reading

1 a it has been deliberately sunk and is used for training
   b where she first tried diving/where the introductory course takes place
   c someone who is your partner on a dive

2 1 D 2 F 3 A 4 G 5 C 6 E

Vocabulary

1. **-ive** informative, argumentative, submissive
   -ious malicious, mysterious, suspicious
   -eous outrageous, advantageous
   -able controllable, memorable
   -ible forcible, possible, terrrible

2. a outrageous
   b argumentative
   c suspicious
   d informative
   e submissive
   f malicious
   g mysterious
   h advantageous
   i memorable

Grammar

1. 1 have been cutting
   2 had previously been covered
   3 has now lost
   4 have been killed
   5 had become/have become
   6 has recently been added
   7 had never (before) shown

2. 1 a a   b no article
   2 a no article b a
   3 a no article b the
   4 a no article b no article
   5 a The   b A
   6 a no article b A
   7 a no article b the

3. 1 a   6 an   11 the
   2 the   7 a   12 -
   3 the   8 -
   4 the   9 the
   5 -   10 the

Listening

2. 1 50/fifty
   2 brain cells
   3 3.2/three point two
   4 small head(s)
   5 life expectancy
   6 rainy
   7 insects
   8 groups

Audio script

On our 'Natural World' slot today, we're taking a look at animals in a slightly different light. We humans tend to think we've got it all sewn up when it comes to athleticism, and events such as the Olympics show just what we can achieve. But what we fail to realise is that in terms of real physical abilities, our counterparts in the animal world leave us standing. Let's begin with brute strength. We're all impressed when we watch someone like an Olympic weight-lifting champion hoisting 1.6 times his own body weight above his head. But one tiny ant can make an Olympic champion look positively puny in comparison. The ant can lift not just double, or even treble, but a staggering 50 times its own weight – no human could match that. And have you any idea just how many brain cells an ant has? Tens, hundreds, thousands? Well, it may surprise you to know that each ant has 250,000 brain cells, so a colony of 40,000 ants actually equals one human being in terms of brain cells!

And what about speed? The fastest man on earth broke the 100 metre world record in 9.58 seconds. But we all know the cheetah can beat this – by 6.38 seconds in fact – with a time of 3.2 seconds. There are several reasons why the animals can do this: one is because of their enlarged heart, liver and lungs, which help to deliver bursts of oxygen and energy, and another is – not as you might think because of their long legs – but because of their small head, which offers little wind resistance. But all this fast-living takes its toll and this seemingly healthy physical exercise does not unfortunately guarantee longevity. Exactly the opposite in fact, because the life expectancy of the cheetah is low, less than ten years to be precise, with many cubs never reaching adulthood.

But let's consider another aspect of physical ability – jumping. Well, two and a half metres seems to be the best we humans can achieve. The springbok, however, jump not to win a medal but for joy when they're with the herd. During the rainy season, this is particularly common to see and when they do this, it's easy to see how they got their name. The creature can manage a jump of 4 metres from a standing start – they don't even need a run-up to jump five times their own height.

And last but not least, there's shooting. The fastest shooter in the natural world is the archer fish. This extraordinary creature can shoot not merely a few centimetres but a 1.5 metre jet out of the water to catch insects. You might argue that an Olympic archer might actually be able to shoot further than his ocean-going counterpart, but he does have to reload more often! And the fish are probably more effective than we humans are because they do it not as individuals or even in pairs but in groups. So, based on the evidence we have in front of us, it is beginning to look as if we need to organise another competition to run alongside all those which will appear in the next Olympic games – namely, the Animal Olympics!

Use of English

1. Patagonia for six weeks

2. 1 deal   5 never/not
   2 away   6 first
   3 enough   7 went
   4 hardly   8 with

3. a one-   e too
   b little   f from
   c long   g put
   d on   h is

Unit 5

Reading

1. a Roger Bannister ran a mile in three minutes, 59 seconds.
   b Bob Beamon set a new record for the long jump of 8.9027 metres.
   c His record was broken.
   d Children competed in several sports rather than just one or two.

2. 1 D 2 B 3 C 4 C 5 A 6 D

Key 99

Vocabulary

1
- a hand
- b foot
- c head
- d tip
- e foot
- f head
- g leg
- h fingers

2
- a head for
- b on the tip of my tongue
- c get his head round
- d cost an arm and a leg
- e give me a hand
- f put your foot in it
- g foot the bill
- h working my fingers to the bone

3
- a survivor, survival
- b performer, performance
- c terrorist, terrorism
- d coordinator, coordination
- e immigrant, immigration
- f defender/defendant, defence
- g coach, coach
- h achiever, achievement

4
- a performances
- b Immigrants
- c terrorism
- d defender
- e survivors
- f coordination
- g achievements
- h coaches

Grammar

1 Suggested answers
1. He said (that) it means (that) he has to keep himself in good physical shape.
2. He told me (that) travelling to remote places …
3. He admitted to always wearing his boots …/He admitted (that) he always wears …
4. He explained that (because) he's very tall …
5. He added that someone in his hut …
6. He went on to say (that) he always carries …
7. He suggested (that) I (could/should) join him …
8. (But he)/He warned me to keep …

2
- a considerate
- b natural
- c correct
- d compatible
- e known
- f suitable
- g flammable

3
- a non-violent
- b impractical
- c incompetent
- d disconnected
- e illegible
- f mistreated
- g unsteady
- h unreasonable
- i non-fiction

Listening

2 1 C 2 B 3 A 4 C 5 B 6 A

Audio script

Extract one
A: You also released a fitness video a few years back, Mary, is that right?
B: That was just after I'd finished filming *The Planet*.
A: Did you enjoy making the video?
B: I loved it! I know it seemed to be the 'in' thing to do at the time – just about everyone was releasing fitness videos. But actually sport and exercise were my first loves! I was a serious athlete long before I went into films. So it was a project that was close to my heart.
A: Well, it was certainly the most successful video of its kind at the time.
B: I'm not sure why it was quite so popular. I think perhaps it was because I connected with the people who were using it. I wasn't trying to be too ambitious or getting them to push themselves too far. I just wanted the people who used the video to have a fun workout when they had the time. It's so important to enjoy keeping fit. Like with everything – if it's a pain to do, you'll find a way to get out of it! Human nature!

Extract two
A: You think people should use lunchtimes as a chance to do something healthy, is that right?
B: Absolutely! It's really important to use lunchtimes profitably – to recharge our batteries for the afternoon ahead.
A: And what would you suggest?
B: One of the best things we can do is to get out of our workplace and have a change of scene. Going for a walk outside is an obvious activity. Get out in the park and get some fresh air in your lungs and sunshine on your skin. Believe it or not our bodies physically need sunshine, and lack of it can affect us mentally as well – sometimes leading to depression. And taking a brisk walk every day, even for 20 minutes, can help prevent back problems occurring. This is becoming more common these days as we're spending so much time inactive, sitting at desks and working on computers.
A: And what if the weather's bad?
B: The important thing is not to just flick through a magazine – do a crossword or a word game – it's great exercise for the brain.

Extract three
A: Quite honestly, I think this campaign for healthy school dinners has been a disaster.
B: That's putting it rather strongly, isn't it? It must have had some positive impact, surely?
A: Not as far as I can see. I know in theory it is a good idea and something has to be done to encourage children to adopt healthier eating habits.
B: Exactly. And now in school cafeterias there isn't a burger in sight! Junk food has disappeared and in its place the kids can eat salads, vegetables, fruit… .
A: That's all very well and good, but look at all the food school cooks are throwing away every day – it's scandalous! Cafeterias are empty and the children are going to the fish and chip shop in their lunch breaks. How healthy is that?! The problem is that the whole campaign went too far, too quickly. Neither the cooks nor the kids were prepared for the change – which you've got to admit has been pretty dramatic!
B: You think we should go back to burgers on the menu?
A: Not at all. We just need to go more slowly.

Use of English

1 b

2
1. membership
2. findings
3. productive
4. energetically
5. reduction
6. beneficial
7. critics
8. intensity

3
a enthusiasm/enthusiast, enthusiastic, enthusiastically
b reduction
c encouragement
d achievement
e increase, increasingly
f significance, significant, significantly
g occurrence
h criticism/critic, critical, critically

4
a argument, judgement
b dramatic, revelations
c romantic, exceptionally

Unit 6

Reading

1 disappointed

2 1 B/E 2 B/E 3 F 4 A 5 C 6 D/E
7 D/E 8 B 9 D 10 E

Vocabulary

1 1 A 2 B 3 C 4 C 5 A

2
1 a giggle, b snigger
2 a mumble, b whisper
3 a overhear, b eavesdrop

Suggested answers
1 unpleasant
2 only a few people can hear
3 secretly listen

3
a eavesdropping
b giggled/were giggling
c mumble

5
1 responsible
2 for questioning
3 my attention
4 extreme views
5 a party
6 the line

6 a 6 b 2 c 3 d 1 e 4 f 5

Grammar

1
a shouldn't   e might
b must   f can't
c should   g ought to
d must

2
b can't have received
c might have been delayed
d may have missed
e must have done
f can't have been

3 a 2 b 3 c 1

4
a needn't have worried
b needn't pay
c needn't arrive
d needn't have spent

Listening

2 1 C 2 B 3 E 4 F 5 A 6 C 7 F
8 E 9 G 10 A

Audio script

Speaker 1
In the 1950s, they carried out some research in America that showed that going without breakfast made you less efficient during the late morning. For years this wasn't challenged until a closer study of the original research showed that the findings hadn't really been proved. More recent research shows that going without breakfast has no measurable effects at all, either mentally or physically. It seems that breakfast is simply a matter of personal preference. As for me, I really need regular meals, starting with breakfast. I burn up so much energy during training that I need the food!

Speaker 2
Clients often ask me about the old saying that carrots help you see in the dark. I can assure you that poor eyesight can only be helped by wearing glasses or with surgery. It has very little to do with nutrition. But it's true that if you're short of vitamin A – which is rare nowadays – you won't see well in dim light: but let's face it, no one can see in the dark! And because carrots contain carotene, which can be converted to vitamin A, they make up for this deficiency, but if you've already got enough, then carrots won't make any difference at all.

Speaker 3
Remember that cartoon character, Popeye, who ate spinach to get super strength and huge muscles? Parents used to tell their kids to do the same! There is some truth in the idea because it's packed with iron – a nutrient that's stored in the muscles. It can be eaten raw but it's more nutritious when it's cooked. It's something I usually try to have on the menu and customers love it! What most people don't realise is that to get the most from it, you should eat it with a fruit or vegetable rich in vitamin C – like oranges – to increase the absorption of the iron.

Speaker 4
Whenever I had a cold, my mother always said 'feed a cold and starve a fever.' I personally don't think there's any real cure for sniffly viruses, other than going to bed and resting. That's the advice the doctors give out in the practice where I work. But I read in a magazine in the waiting room that there's some truth in this old wives' tale. Apparently, eating a meal boosts the immune system that destroys viruses, which cause colds. What they haven't discovered is whether particular foods have beneficial effects. But come to think of it, it's true that when you have a fever, you just don't feel hungry.

Speaker 5
I'm not that keen on fish but I was told it makes you brainy, so I always forced myself to eat it at exam time! I must admit I find myself recommending it to my pupils when their exams are approaching. I've read that oily fish like mackerel are all good sources of omega-3 fats (which of course don't make you fat) and they help the development of the brain both before birth and after. So if you're someone who loves fish, the good news is that it can help your brain function. Thankfully, it doesn't actually improve your intelligence, so I don't have to eat it!

Key 101

Use of English

1 A giant mirror was erected on a mountain to reflect sunlight into the village during the winter months.

2 1 B 2 A 3 B 4 D 5 B 6 C
7 B 8 A

Review Units 4–6

1 a put my foot in it
b head for
c give me a hand
d working your fingers to the bone
e It's on the tip of my tongue

2 The students **became** aware … when they **started** some research … It **appeared** that the lynx **had been** threatened … their numbers **have been** depleted and their natural habitat **has been** decreasing.

3 a counterfeit   d take
b count   e whispering
c eavesdropped on f giggling

4 a attention
b line
c responsible
d questioning
e party

5 a unsteady
b non-violent
d imprecise
f unnatural
g disorganised
h misunderstood
i mispronounced

6 Jane Henley **could not have been** happier … Her parents **must** have been … It **can't** have been … they needn't have **worried**!

7 1 A: no article
       B: no article, no article
2 A: no article, the
   B: no article, a
3 A: the, the, the
   B: the
4 A: no article, the
   B: no article

5 A: no article, the
   B: the
6 A: no article
   B: the
7 A: a
   B: the
8 A: the
   B: The

8 suspicious, informative, courteous, malicious, outrageous
a courteous
b informative
c malicious
d suspicious
e outrageous

9 Suggested answers
a Sarah admitted that ever since she had been a child, she had been desperate to travel.
b She asked Ted if he had ever been on a safari.
c He told her that he hadn't.
d But added that it was one of his ambitions.
e She went on to say that she hoped (that) one day he would go on a safari.
f She offered him a place on her next trip.

10 a offered to give me/said he would give me
b was taken in by
c get my head round

Unit 7

Reading

1 during the English Civil War/in the 17th century

2 1 A 2 B 3 C 4 C

Vocabulary

1 1 cut off   4 called off
2 bring … off   5 took off
3 showing off

2 a 4 b 2 c 5 d 1 e 3

3 1 take it in   4 brought in
2 show … in   5 cuts in
3 called in

4 a 4 b 2 c 1 d 5 e 3

5 a off b in c off d in e in

Grammar

1 1 Lying
2 being located/located
3 Buried
4 Receiving
5 not seeing/not having seen
6 known
7 searching

2 a -ee
b -ship
c -ess (actress)
d -hood (likelihood)
e -ness (happiness)
f -ist
g -less/ful
h -ese (Chinese, Portuguese, Lebanese)

3 Group g can take -less and -ful.

4 a politician   g Democracy
b contentment   h argument
c anxiety   i technician
d musician   j secrecy
e clarity   k authenticity
f fulfilment   l diplomacy

Listening

1 a manuscript
b Gluck

2 1 extra cash
2 fake
3 decades
4 blue
5 auction house
6 own hand
7 grandfather
8 generation

Audio script

Searching dusty attics for hidden treasures has become a national pastime in some countries, no doubt encouraged by the popularity of many TV antique programmes or just the desire to make some extra cash! All of us are becoming increasingly aware that items we've found may actually be quite valuable or at least worth more than just a few pounds. People everywhere it seems are clearing out their attics, cupboards, garages, wherever, and taking what they find to be valued. The upside of this is that there are a lot of tidy houses! But what have you really found? Is that picture you're convinced is a Rembrandt really a Rembrandt? The downside of all this searching is that it could result in finding a fake and nothing more. However, having said that, some people do strike lucky. Back in 1990, a librarian in southern California was clearing out her attic when she discovered the original first half of *Huckleberry Finn* by Mark Twain! The story goes that a set of old trunks, full of paper, had been sitting in her attic for decades. She had inherited them from her aunt but had never got round to investigating them. So, one day she finally decided to get rid of all the clutter and while checking through the trunks she found a fragile package wrapped in brown wrapping paper. On opening it she found lots of blue paper covered in writing in black and purple ink. It was the original manuscript of *Huckleberry Finn*, well, the first half anyway. I imagine the librarian nearly passed out!

So, what would you do in this situation? The librarian contacted the world-famous auction house Sotheby's and faxed them copies of the pages. Sotheby's then confirmed the find and they had it rushed to New York in an armoured car! They were ecstatic! The manuscript, totalling 665 pages, contained passages not included in the final version of the book and corrections, all of which were written in Mark Twain's own hand. They called it 'the most extraordinary literary discovery of the post-war period'.

The history of the manuscript was traced. It seems that Twain had sent the manuscript to the librarian's grandfather, James Gluck, who was a collector of original manuscripts. They found a letter acknowledging receipt of the manuscript. Unfortunately Gluck caught pneumonia a short time after receiving it and died. Upset by his death, the family packed away all his papers without checking through them. They were eventually inherited by one of his daughters and stored in trunks in her attic until the next generation and the librarian eventually made the find. So, there are treasures out there – amongst all the rubbish and the clutter. Keep looking. Who knows what you'll find?

Use of English

1 The terracotta army is famous because the figures are more than two thousand years old and are incredibly detailed.

2
1 emperor
2 accidentally
3 excavations
4 burial
5 assassinate
6 arrangements
7 warriors
8 unmistakable

3
a fame
b powerful
c reign
d explanation
e building
f detailed
g figuratively
h watchful
i credibility
j continuity/continuation

Unit 8

Reading

1 He expresses some hope in the the final paragraph, but generally the author does not appear to be optimistic.

2 1 C   2 B   3 B   4 C   5 A   6 D

Vocabulary

1 a 4   b 1   c 5   d 3   e 6   f 2
Suggested answers
self-motivated, self-opinionated, self-righteous, self-service, self-sufficient

2
a full-time/part-time
b left-handed
c light-hearted
d narrow-minded
e handmade
f overstated

3 b in   c im   d ir   e in
   f un   g im   h un

4 1 e 2 g 3 f 4 h 5 c 6 b 7 a 8 d

5
a indistinguishable
b unsociable
c unbearable
d inaccessible
e sensitive/insecure
f irreversible/unchangeable
g immeasurable
h insensitive/uncaring

Grammar

1 Suggested answers
a will hear
b hadn't taken/tried to take
c could call
d could reach
e might be able to find

2
a If my aunt hadn't lent me the money, I wouldn't have been able to go abroad.
b If you stay out in the midday sun, you'll get burned.
c If Thomas hadn't had three jobs over the summer, he wouldn't have been able to buy a motorbike.
d If I were to offer you a scholarship, how would you feel about it?
e If demand for our products were not falling, profits would not be down.

3
a ignites/is ignited, goes up/will go up
b knew, would tell
c would have gained, had volunteered
d hadn't been, would have left
e Let, 'd like
f hadn't worked, wouldn't have got
g hadn't argued, had kept, wouldn't have got

Key 103

Listening

2 1 B 2 D 3 C 4 B 5 C 6 D

Audio script

I: Today I welcome Paul Williams, who's an expert in artificial intelligence, or 'AI', as it's known. Paul – let's start with a forward-looking question. How difficult is it to predict the future of artificial intelligence?
P: Well, I'll answer that one by actually looking backwards. It's interesting that in the 1940s, a man called Thomas Watson, head of the company IBM at the time, famously predicted that the world demand for computers might be as many as five. And in the 1950s, AI researchers predicted that a computer would be the world chess champion by 1968 – but that took a few more decades. AI's certainly had its share of wacky predictions!
I: But leaving aside the predictions of the past, what would be your appraisal of AI's future?
P: There's still a lot of controversy about all this. But basically, most experts remain optimistic about its future. Nevertheless, they're currently predicting that it won't be until the middle of this century that intelligent machines will be present in most areas of our lives.
I: OK. So what's the impact of AI now?
P: Well, as you may know, every text message and email you send is routed using AI. And there are many other examples of what you would call 'narrow AI' – that's something which can now be done by a computer, but which used to be done manually. It's called 'narrow' because it is within a specific area, but it's actually getting wider.
I: So is this an unprecedented leap forward?
P: Some people would say that the best comparison is probably that AI is at the same stage now as the personal computer industry was in 1978. There wasn't a lot of choice back then. And, obviously, they couldn't do as much as today's computers do. But my take on the situation is that the comparison with the early computer industry doesn't give a true picture of AI's successes. It's already used in very advanced ways, like scheduling flights or reading X-rays. And the best is surely to come.
I: What do you mean exactly?

P: Well, I think that in the next few decades we'll have a much better understanding of how the human brain works. That will give us a sort of template to follow and it'll really help in developing AI. That would mean that within the next fifty years, there'll be a lot of intelligent robots. You may say that it all sounds a bit far-fetched, but take a moment to think back to the 1900s. Who would have thought that a century later, it would be normal to have computers in your home – and I'm not just talking about laptops or personal computers. You only have to look at the computer chips in our coffee makers, refrigerators and dishwashers to see the kind of unexpected leaps that took place.
I: So should we be afraid of what these intelligent machines might soon do to us?
P: The thought of a hyper-intelligent coffee maker trying to kill us all seems a little far-fetched! What we should perhaps be more worried about is whether we humans will be made redundant by a legion of intelligent machines. But the simple answer is that we won't wake up one morning to find our lives dominated by artificially intelligent devices.
I: How can you be so sure?
P: Well, science fiction is just that – fiction; it's not based on fact. Spielberg's film *AI* may have had a company designing a robot that could bond like a human, but that was in a film. But scientists don't just suddenly decide to make an emotional, human-like robot. Things don't happen that way. Some of these innovations take many years to perfect. The road from here to the real application of artificial intelligence will take thousands of different routes. There's really no need to panic.
I: Paul, thanks very much …

Use of English

1 People want to get onto a course or into a workplace, and to develop 'soft skills'. Businesses want to raise their profile in the community.

2 1 A 2 B 3 C 4 C 5 C 6 A 7 B 8 A

3 1 A 2 C 3 D 4 B 5 C 6 B

Unit 9

Reading

1 A Scotland   D USA
   B England   E England
   C Cuba   F USA

2 1 B 2 A 3 C 4 F 5 E 6 C 7 F 8 B 9 D 10 A

Vocabulary

1 a for   e behind
   b back on   f off
   c over (oneself) g out with
   d through

2 1 fallen behind
   2 falling over themselves
   3 fall back on
   4 fell through
   5 fell out
   6 fell for
   7 fallen off

Grammar

1 Bowlands Academy of Arts was established five years ago. The establishment has now been officially recognised by the Department of Education. A programme of short, intensive courses, as well as three-year degree courses, are offered to students. A range of examinations can be taken (by students) throughout the year. Students are instructed in small groups (by staff) and a personal tutor is assigned to every student. Accommodation in a hall of residence must be booked in advance (by anyone requiring it). A deposit needs to be enclosed with the enrolment form. The balance will be requested (by the Academy) before the course starts. The Academy needs to be informed immediately if students intend to withdraw from their course.

2
1. get your eyes tested
2. had her ears pierced
3. get the/your jacket dry-cleaned
4. get confiscated
5. had the car serviced
6. doesn't get stolen
7. am having the matter investigated

3
a. It is rumoured that the government is going to resign.
b. Interest rates are predicted to rise by financial experts.
c. The missing gangland leader was assumed to have been murdered.
d. It is thought (that) the plane crash was due to human error.
e. Terrorists are believed to be hiding out in the north of the country.

Listening

2 1 A 2 B 3 C 4 A 5 C 6 B

Audio script

Extract one
A: This new punishment policy seems to be succeeding but it has certainly attracted a lot of media attention.
B: Yes – that's true. There's been a fair amount of controversy surrounding it. But there will always be people for and against different forms of punishment. This particular idea is proving very effective.
A: Why do people call it 'the cooler room'?
B: Well, it's an isolation unit and I suppose people see it as a place for schoolchildren to cool off. 'The cooler room' also featured in the film *The Great Escape* where it was a room used to punish the prisoners.
A: So, what happens in 'the cooler room'?
B: Disruptive pupils are sent there to do work away from their friends and they aren't allowed to leave without permission. Food and drink are brought into the room and they're constantly observed through a window. They can be sent there for as little as one hour but for really bad behaviour it can be up to three schooldays! They hate being away from their mates and this is what makes it effective.

Extract two
A: At the time they were introduced, ASBOs seemed a really good idea – a form of punishment that targets people guilty of habitual antisocial behaviour and forbids them to do certain things, associate with certain people or go to certain places. That's got to be better than sending them to prison. Well, that was the thinking anyway.
B: But these recent statistics are pretty alarming, wouldn't you say? It appears that ASBOs aren't having the effect that government thought they would.
A: You're right. What's happening is that a lot of the kids don't actually understand the limitations of the orders and those that do understand don't particularly care. In some cases it's developed into a game to see how often they can breach their order, ignoring all the restrictions, and get away with it.
B: The report says that ASBOs are even seen as a 'badge of honour'.
A: I know! Rather like a symbol – something to show off about and be proud of. So, you see in one way they're encouraging antisocial behaviour rather than discouraging it!

Extract three
A: Could you tell our listeners exactly what the Witness Support Programme does?
B: Certainly. We do a lot of different types of work but mainly we're concerned with supporting people who have been victims, or witnesses, to crimes. In particular, we help when cases go to trial and they are required to attend court to give evidence.
A: And why do these people need help at court?
B: You can imagine the trauma they have suffered, then having to relive this and describe what happened when they give evidence. Standing up in court can be an unnerving experience. We try to make it less stressful. We bring them to the court, prior to the trial, to familiarise them with the surroundings and the procedures. Then, during the trial, we provide a separate room away from the public and the risk of meeting the friends and family of the accused person.
A: This support programme is a charity, isn't it?
B: Yes. In this area, three of us are paid to organise everything but we depend on large numbers of volunteers who help the witnesses along the way.

Use of English

1 crime/drama/thriller

2
1. like
2. who
3. from
4. Even
5. or
6. no/little
7. over/across
8. enough

3
a. chances are (that) you won't/will not
b. came up against
c. being looked into
d. haven't/have not paid back

Review Units 7–9

1 1 d 2 e 3 c 4 b 5 c/d 6 f 7 c

2
1. Having peered
2. Using
3. identifying
4. known
5. making
6. Having concluded

3
a. fallen for
b. fall behind
c. falling over themselves
d. fell through
e. fell out
f. fall for

4
a. employee
b. friendships
c. childhood
d. actress
e. neighbourhood
f. careless

5
a. fallen out
b. have gone off
c. fall behind
d. told off
e. take in
f. fall back on
g. took off

6
a. take in
b. show off
c. call in
d. take off
e. bring in
f. cut in
g. bring off

Key 105

7
1 in f
2 ir h
3 un d
4 in g
5 un b
6 im a
7 im c
8 im e

8
a had
b asks
c had left
d read
e see
f had visited
g wasn't
h hadn't bought

9
a contentment
b anxious
c clear
d secrecy
e diplomatic
f authenticity
g democratic

10
a arrived
b is being given
c is thought
d is considered to be
e being made
f has been
g could have been

11
a are always cut off
b went up in flames
c have/get your eyes tested

Unit 10

Reading

2 1 C 2 A 3 G 4 D 5 F 6 E

Vocabulary

1
1 a fares, b fees
2 a receipt, b bill
3 a wage, b salary
4 a cash, change

2
a Wages
b fees
c change
d receipt

3
a falsify
b strengthen
c activate
d broaden
e typify
f alternate
g demonstrate
h sadden
i pacify

4
a strengthened
b activate
c falsified
d alternated
e pacify
f saddened
g broaden

Grammar

1
a unless all safety regulations are complied with.
b provided/as long as you are honest with me now.
c unless it's an emergency.
d supposing I wanted you to be involved in it.
e unless he'd been forced to.

2 1 a 2 b 3 b 4 b 5 a 6 b 7 b

3
a The whole
b hardly any
c one
d None
e Each
f little
g Loads
h others
i a few
j most

Listening

2 1 B 2 C 3 C 4 C 5 B 6 D

Audio script

I: Sam, this issue of music piracy is a very complicated one, isn't it?
Sam: It certainly is and for one main reason. Firstly, just to clarify the situation, it's all about firms creating software for distributing songs and films on the Internet without any royalties being paid to the artists or anyone else involved in the production. These firms are being taken to court but they aren't the ones downloading the songs and films – they only manufacture the software. I suppose a good comparison would be if there was, say, an outbreak of robberies, should the police be chasing the manufacturers of the ladders or the tools the thieves used to commit the robberies, or should they be chasing the thieves themselves?
I: So, is there is a legal precedent – any other cases like these which have taken place in a court of law?
Sam: Well, interestingly enough, back in 1984, the entertainment industry tried and failed to legally block the manufacturers of video recorders because they could be used to make pirate copies of films. The judge ruled that a manufacturer couldn't be held responsible for the use to which its products were put. It's close, although not exactly parallel, with this current case. Apart from anything else, it wasn't clear that the overwhelming use of video recorders would be for piracy – in other words, making illegal copies of films. So it all came to nothing.
I: So what's different about this week's case?
Sam: I think it all hinges on how much a product can be used illegally as opposed to legally. Just going back to the robbers for a moment, who would seriously expect ladders to be banned because a minority of people use them illegally? It just doesn't make sense, does it? I think most people would agree that manufacturers who produce software used primarily for distributing copyrighted works are in a different position because that work should legally be paid for and earn artists money.
I: So who's right? What's your view on the subject?
Sam: That's not an easy one to answer. If the music industry gets its way, you could argue that this might block the development of technology used to download music and films. Anyone involved in developing new technology in this field would be put off by the threats of lawsuits from film and music companies who argue that the invention could allow people to download songs or films for free. And we all know that if free music is available, people will take it whatever the rights or wrongs. But my biggest worry is that if artists don't get paid, they'll be less likely to perform. And where will that leave us? We'll be left without an entertainment industry.
I: But have you talked to members of the public about this?
Sam: I've done a lot of interesting research into this quite recently. One of the most popular reactions has been this: it's time for the entertainment industry to look into new methods of distribution. It needs to make distribution costs lower and produce cheaper products for the public. There seems to be a general feeling that because the copyright laws are so strict, the entertainment industry is making a fortune while the general public is being ripped off, as it were.
I: Do you think it's worse in the film industry?
Sam: There is a problem with films. Currently, most titles are released in the US first, before transferring across the Atlantic to Europe and the rest of the world. This leads to movies recorded on camcorder in a US cinema appearing on

the Internet within a matter of days. Once a film's been released everywhere and in every medium, illegal copies cease to be in big demand. So maybe the answer is that all films should be released on the big screen in every country across the world at the same time.

I: Thanks, Sam, we'll just have to wait and see what happens next …

Use of English

1 A website where people give away unwanted items. It started as a list on the Internet.

2
1 impulsive
2 unwanted
3 promotion
4 valuable
5 environmentalist
6 global
7 reporters
8 reasonably

3
a irresistible, resistance
b inefficient, efficiency
c freedom, freely
d reusable/useful, useless
e explanations, explanatory

Unit 11

Reading

1 their personal experience of photography

2 1 B 2 A 3 D 4 B

Vocabulary

1
a look   d stand   g leading
b live   e felt   h wake
c face   f get

2 1 a 2 e 3 f 4 d
5 g 6 c 7 b 8 h

3
1 put down to, put up with
2 get away with, come down with
3 drop in on, drop out of

4
a put down to
b after the particles

5
a put up with
b put (it) down to
c come down with
d get away with
e dropped out of
f drop in on

Grammar

1
a … and just **like** all the others.
b … it was by far the **worst** choice.
c She's a lot **like** her sister.
d the **less** I want to settle down …
e It's far **more** interesting …
f It was **nowhere** near …

2
a slightly   e nowhere
b just   f nothing
c nearly   g bit
d no more   h great

4
a such   d so   g so
b so   e so
c such   f such

5 1 a 2 g 3 d 4 c,f 5 b 6 e

Listening

2
1 1800/eighteen hundred
2 (past) traditions
3 arrive early
4 comfortable shoes
5 spotlights
6 security
7 standing back
8 unusual

Audio script

Ever felt baffled by modern art? Well, if you learn the tricks, you can fake a level of expertise easily. Faking art appreciation is not difficult, and I'll tell you how to do it. Who knows, you might even pick up a bit of genuine appreciation along the way. The last two centuries have seen many movements in modern art. Don't worry about that; just realise that art that doesn't obviously try to reflect reality is usually considered 'modern'. Modern Art began around 1800, a century before Picasso and his friends revived it in the 1900s. There was a growing movement of artists trying to break away from traditions. So what makes a work 'modern' is the breaking away from these traditions; those who did that got the headlines. And remember that modern art doesn't necessarily represent concrete objects but delights in its own strangeness.

Once you've understood that, it's time to visit an art gallery. The most important thing you should do is arrive early. You want to see the works of art, not the back of someone's head. Also, remember not to wear smart footwear – wear comfortable shoes – you could easily walk a couple of kilometres in a gallery.

The next question is what to do when standing in front of a work of art. First, stand in the right place – it's different for each work, so try a few different positions to see what works best. Don't stand where spotlights make a glare on the painting. If you see people crouched on the floor peering up, join them in trying to find that glare-free corner. It'll prove that you really are analysing the painting instead of looking at it.

Don't forget that art can be priceless, and protecting it is a serious issue for galleries. Security is therefore strict – avoid leaning over the ropes; if you get too close to the art, you might be thrown out. And no matter what, never touch the art unless a sign specifically says you can. Remember that you may harm the work by doing so. I know it sounds ridiculous, but take a pair of binoculars. Sometimes you can get a better view by standing back and looking through binoculars than by wrestling your way to the front of the crowd.

And, don't waste time in front of mediocre works. Look for something unusual. Even in the best gallery, not everything is great. And if it doesn't interest you, pass it by. And if someone asks you why you don't like a painting, just say something like, 'the artist obviously didn't take into account the subject's emotional state'. Nobody will argue.

So, that's it. If you commit all this to memory, the next time you go to a gallery, you'll be able to appreciate the art.

Use of English

1 The paintings have remained hidden since 1969/they were created.

2
1 in   5 no one/nobody
2 more   6 there
3 under   7 such
4 until   8 at

3 a got round to finalising
   b in the event of
   c to get away with
   d went on to become

Unit 12

Reading

1 c

2 1 E 2 D 3 B/C 4 B/C 5 B 6 A
   7 C 8 A/E 9 A/E 10 D

Vocabulary

1 1 B 2 A 3 C 4 A
   5 C 6 A 7 B 8 A

2 a 5 had set/set   d 3 sets
   b 4 sets   e 2 wasn't set
   c 1 has set

3 1 a decline   b refused
   2 a rejected   b refute
   3 a denied   b disallowed
   4 a oppose   b resisted

Grammar

1 a 4 b 2 c 6 d 3
   e 1 f 7 g 5

2 Suggested answers
   a Under no circumstances will I resign.
   b Hardly/Scarcely had they finished eating when the doorbell rang.
      No sooner had they finished eating than the doorbell rang.
   c Little did we realise/know that we were living next to a notorious criminal.
   d Nowhere can I find a copy of that book.
   e Only when I saw how cheap the car was did I decide to buy it.

3 a Pat is not tall enough to be a professional dancer.
   b There are far too few people using public transport nowadays.
   c The training course is not cheap enough for most people to consider enrolling.
   d I'm too young to drive.
   e He didn't speak slow(ly) enough for me to hear what he said.

4 a If the tea is not hot **enough** …
   b I'm **too** young …
   c There's **too** much poverty …
   d Is there **enough** time …
   e … far **too** complicated?
   f … studying hard **enough**
   g … **enough** experience to …
   h Please speak clearly **enough** …

Listening

2 1 C 2 E 3 B 4 D 5 G
   6 G 7 B 8 E 9 C 10 F

Audio script

Speaker 1
Of course, I'm not going to deny that governments have a huge responsibility to protect the planet. But the single, most important statement I would like to hear governments making is that the science of global warming is not an exact one – not as long as various methods of measuring temperatures give contradictory results. Over the last 25 years, weather satellites have shown little, if any warnings, and computer models used to predict future temperatures and other climate effects have produced completely different predictions that can't be relied on. It would be crazy to use inaccurate information as a basis for policies that could have an effect on national economies.

Speaker 2
The one measure I would like to see governments agreeing on and promoting would be to introduce legislation forcing producers and manufacturers to clearly show the environmental cost of transporting goods. Consumers everywhere should be able to see at a glance exactly what they're doing to the environment by flying in a plane, for example. Showing people that they can make different lifestyle choices and purchases is one essential step towards reflecting the damage to the environment. So the environmental damage caused by transporting, say, fresh fruit and vegetables around the world should be made clear – just like the damage caused by taking a package holiday and flying to your destination. It's only by doing this that you can make people realise the short and long-term effects of what they're doing.

Speaker 3
Science has already demonstrated that climate change is happening – but there are still many unanswered questions that need detailed scientific research. These include: What are the likely environmental and human impacts? What exactly are the regional changes going to be? How are extreme events going to change, for example, flooding, heat waves and drought? These questions can only be answered through continued coordinated research. And that costs money. So my request would be that governments invest much more in doing research in this field.

Speaker 4
My worry is that governments are not focusing enough on adaptation. True, they all make statements about cutting greenhouse gas emissions. But what they fail to realise is that climate change is occurring and it's going to carry on occurring even if we do cut emissions. We already know that sea levels are rising and there are heatwaves now in countries like the UK. So what I want governments to do is admit that they need to bring in global legislation which will help to minimise what is going on at this moment in time.

Speaker 5
The point is that the developed world created the present problems with the environment as it became industrialised and wealthy. So I think that governments have to recognise the fact that developing countries will need more energy as their standards of living rise – and that if those needs are met in the easiest and cheapest way, their greenhouse gas emissions would be enormously high. So we have an obligation to help developing countries avoid a repetition of what happened to us. And the developing countries must play their part in protecting the planet as their economies grow.

108 Key

Use of English

1 Suggested answers
an environmental group/local recycling group/supermarkets, to encourage people to reuse plastic bags and avoid unnecessary waste

2 1 C 2 B 3 B 4 D 5 A 6 C 7 A 8 B

Review Units 10–12

1
a nothing like as warm as
b under no circumstances will
c had the ability

2
a Mexican food is far spicier than British food./British food is far more bland than Mexican food.
b The summer temperature in France is only slightly warmer than it is in Britain./The summer temperature in Britain is only slightly colder than it is in France.
c Extreme sports are a great deal more exciting than racket sports./Racket sports are a great deal more boring than extreme sports.
d This exercise is a bit more difficult than the others./The other exercises are a bit less difficult than this exercise.

3
a The film was brilliant but far too long.
b Do you think we have allowed enough time to finish the project?
c We haven't thought this problem through carefully enough.
d The company has already invested too much money in this new venture.
e I'm afraid your application arrived too late for you to be considered.

4
1 money   4 wages   7 cash
2 change 5 bills
3 salary 6 fares

5
a No sooner had James finished cooking than his sister arrived.
b Little did I know that he had overheard my phonecall to the bank.
c Scarcely had the plane landed on the narrow runway when the passengers began to cheer.
d Nowhere in the city will you find a park as beautiful as Central Park/this (one).
e Only when the politician mentioned taxes was there a cry of protest from the audience.
f Hardly had I reached home when the heavens opened.

6
a live up to
b feel up to
c put up with
d come down with
e drop in on
f put, down to
g come up with

7
a had joined
b don't make a noise
c would stop/had stopped
d had told
e hadn't been driving/hadn't driven
f happens

8
a positioned   d decided
b takes place   e become solid
c enforce

9
a so   e so
b such   f so
c such   g such
d so

10
a refused   e denied
b ensure   f assured
c refuted   g oppose
d ascertain h insure

Speaking

Quick quiz

1 15

2 Part 1 c
Part 2 a
Part 3 b
Part 4 d

3 a 3 b 4 c 2 d 1

4
a Grammatical
b Lexical Resource
c Discourse Management
d Pronunciation
e Interactive Communication

Part 1

1 a, c, d, f
(b) is typical of a Part 2 question
(e) is typical of a Part 3 question

2
1 appropriate
2 interrupt
3 long
4 one
5 Expand
6 Speak
7 eye contact

Part 2

1 True: b, c, e
False: a (you talk about only two pictures)
d (you should begin speaking immediately)
f (you have about 30 seconds for this part of the task)

2
1 both
2 which/that
3 In
4 hand
5 must/could/might/may
6 even/much/a lot/considerably
7 who/that
8 like/such as
9 as

Parts 3 and 4

1
- a two
- b oral instructions and written prompts
- c 15
- d two
- e the whole
- f does not take
- g shouldn't
- h don't see
- i are
- j don't need to

2 a 8 b 3 c 4 d 5 e 2 f 7 g 6 h 1

oxfordenglishtesting.com

What is on the Workbook MultiROM?

The MultiROM in this Workbook Pack has two parts.
- You can listen to the audio material that accompanies the workbook by playing the MultiROM in an audio CD player, or in a media player on your computer.
- You can also access a complete practice test online with the MultiROM. The test comes with instant marking, feedback, tips, a dictionary look-up, and many other features. To find out how to access the test, read this page.

How do I use my MultiROM?

You will find your practice test on a website called oxfordenglishtesting.com. The website contains many different practice tests, including the one that you have access to. Because the practice test is on the internet you will need:
- to be connected to the internet when you use the test
- to have an email address (so that you can register).

When you're ready to try out your practice test for the first time follow these steps:
1 Turn on your computer.
2 Connect to the internet. (If you have a broadband connection, you will probably already be online.)
3 Put the MultiROM into the CD drive of your computer.
4 A screen will appear giving you two options. Single click to access your test.

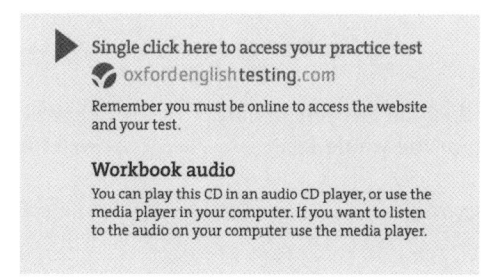

> **Single click here to access your practice test**
> oxfordenglishtesting.com
> Remember you must be online to access the website and your test.
>
> **Workbook audio**
> You can play this CD in an audio CD player, or use the media player in your computer. If you want to listen to the audio on your computer use the media player.

What do I do when I get to the website?

After a few moments your internet browser will open and take you directly to the Welcome page on the website. Follow the steps below.

1 Choose a language from the drop-down list and click **Go**. All pages, apart from the actual practice test, will be in the language you choose.

2 Click on the **Register now** button and fill in the details on the registration form. You will need to give an email address and make up a password. You will need your email address and password every time you log into the system. If you are already registered, click on the **Log in** button.

3 After filling in the registration form click on **Register**. To confirm your registration, click on **Save registration details**. Click on **My tests** where you will be asked to log in. You have 365 days to use the practice test before you have to submit it for final marking.

4 If you have a problem using your MultiROM, go to www.oxfordenglishtesting.com/unlock. You will be asked to click **Register now** if you are a new user. You will then be asked to fill in a registration form and to enter an unlock code. You can find the unlock code printed on your MultiROM. It will look like this 9219e6-9471d9-cf7c79-a5143b. Each code is unique.

Once you have registered, you can access your test in future by going to oxfordenglishtesting.com and logging in. Remember you will need your email and password to log in. You must also be online to do your practice test.

What are the features of an online practice test?

Exam tips	You can see a tip on how to answer every question type.
Dictionary look-up	You can look up the meaning of any word in the practice test using the *Oxford Advanced Learner's Dictionary*. Type the word in the box on the screen to see the definition. You will need to have pop-up windows enabled.
Instant marking and feedback	When you've answered a question, you can mark it straight away to see whether you got it right or wrong, and you can get **Feedback** to find out why.
Change your answer or try again	You can then go back and try to answer the question again as many times as you like. Understanding why you answered a question incorrectly helps you think more clearly about a similar question next time.
Save and come back later	You don't have to complete a Paper at one time. When you log out, it saves what you've done. You can come back to it at any time. You have 365 days before you have to submit the practice test for final marking. The **My tests** page tells you when the test expires.
Mark individual answers, a part, a paper, or the whole test	However much you've done of the practice test, you can mark it and see how well you're doing.
Audio scripts	These are available for all parts of the Listening test. Reading the **Audio script** will help you understand any areas you didn't understand when you were listening.
Sample answers for questions in the Writing paper	You can see **Sample answers** after you've written your own. They've been written by real students, and will give you a good idea of what's expected. What you write will not be marked automatically. If you would like your teacher to mark it, you can print it off to give to them or email it to them. When they've marked it, you can enter the mark on your **Results** page. It does not matter if you do not enter a mark for the writing tasks. The final marks will be adjusted to take that into account.
Useful phrases for the Speaking paper	You get sample Speaking papers and **Useful language** to help you practise offline. You can print the Speaking paper from the **Resources** page, and ask your teacher to do the Speaking paper with you. As with the Writing paper, you can enter the mark your teacher gives you. However, if you don't, your final marks will be adjusted to take that into account.
Results page	Remember this is a practice test, not the real exam. You will see your score by paper and part and as a percentage. Your final score on the practice test is only an indication of how you might perform in the real exam.
Try a sample test first	You can try out a short version of a practice test on oxfordenglishtesting.com before you do a real one. This lets you find out how to use a test before you start.